To Paul

Best Wishes

Mike Ingram

The Battle of Northampton

1460

By Mike Ingram

Published By Northampton Battlefields Society

First published 2015 by Northampton Battlefields Society

© Northampton Battlefields Society, 2015

Cover paintings and maps by Matthew Ryan.

http://matthewryanhistoricalillustrator.com

Editing and digitisation by Nicky Fitzmaurice

http://www.satinpaperbacks.com/

ISBN No: 978-0-9930777-9-1

ISBN No: 978-0-9930777-8-4

Foreword

Northampton today is, frankly, an under-appreciated, often overlooked, town. The joke is, people only know of Northamptonshire because they shoot through it on the M1: they note the name of the county town on notice boards from exits 15 to 16. But this was, once, one of the great centres of power and influence in early and Medieval England. It was also, with Oxford, home to one of the first two universities in the land. Mike Ingram brings fine scholastic research to play, in reminding people of Northampton's past importance - strategic and social. His energetic prose gives colour to every page, while his revelations intrigue and entertain. He helps us appreciate why one of the great battles of English history took place in this Midland town, and he skilfully resurrects the generals and ordinary soldiers who clashed in an engagement that helped lay the foundations of this nation's past. You don't need to be a champion or resident of Northampton to appreciate this overdue appraisal of the battle that bears its name. This is a book that everyone who loves History - particularly the almost forgotten kind - will savour.

Earl Charles Spencer DL

Herein may be seen noble chyvalrye, curtoseye, humanitye, friendlynesse, hardynesse, love, frendship, cowardyse, murdre, hate, virtue, and synne.

William Caxton's preface to Sir Thomas Malory's ' Morte d'Arthur, 1485

Acknowledgements

A massive thank you to Joan Beretta, Nicky Fitzmaurice and Graham Evans who gave their valuable time to give advice and sort out my errors and omissions. Thanks also go to Earl Spencer for his foreword; to Livia Visser-Fuchs of the Richard III Society for her new analysis and translation of Wavrin, and to Matthew Ryan for his brilliant artwork. We must also thank those organisations who gave financial support especially Northamptonshire County Council and Northampton Borough Council who helped through their empowerment funding, and to the committee of Northampton Battlefield Society who also helped make this book possible. We must also give a special thank you to the members of the Society, organisations such as the Battlefields Trust, and those members of the public who continue to support and help protect this important piece of our forgotten national heritage.

Contents

Page

Maps, Charts and Illustrations

Timeline

1450		Jack Cade's rebellion
1452		Richard of York's first rebellion
1455	22 May	1st Battle of St. Albans
1459	Jan	Papal envoy Francesco Coppini arrives in England
	23 Sept	Battle of Blore Heath
	13 Oct	Ludford Bridge – The Yorkist flee to Calais and Ireland
	Nov	The Duke of Somerset attacks Calais
	20 Nov	The Parliament of Devils opens in Coventry
	Dec	Coppini is promoted to Legate
1460	15 Jan	Yorkist raid on Sandwich. The Woodvilles are taken prisoner.
	Jan	King Henry goes on a progress of the East Midlands
	23 April	Somerset is beaten in a battle at Newnham Bridge, near Calais
	18 June	King Henry returns to Coventry
	Mid-June	Coppini is in Calais
	26 June	Fauconberg captures Sandwich
	27 June	The main Yorkist army lands at Sandwich
	2 July	The Yorkists reach London
	4 July	Fauconberg leaves London
	5 July	Main Yorkist army leaves London
	7 July	Lancastrian Army arrives in Northampton
	10 July	**Battle of Northampton**
	13 July	King Henry is taken to London
	9 Sept	Richard of York returns from Ireland
	11 Oct	Richard of York lays claim to the throne of England for the first time
	25 Oct	The Act of Accord is agreed in Parliament
	30 Dec	Battle of Wakefield. York is killed.
1461	2 Feb	Battle of Mortimer's Cross. Yorkist victory
	17 Feb	2nd Battle of St. Albans. Lancastrian Victory
	29 March	Battle of Towton. Yorkist victory
	28 June	Edward, Earl of March, crowned King Edward IV

Medieval Northampton

From the Saxons through to the Wars of the Roses, Northampton and Northamptonshire have played a key part in the country's development. For most of its history the town was a Royal borough, paying a fixed fee to the King.

In Anglo-Saxon times the town prospered as a river port and trading centre, and was home to a Viking army. Although the burh was strong enough to withstand an assault by King Olaf of York in 941, it was burnt in 1010 by a Danish army under the command of Thorkil 'the Tall'. It was burnt again in 1065 by the rebellious northern earls Edwin and Morcar as part of their revolt against the then Earl of Northumbria, Tostig.

By the time of William the Conqueror's great survey of 1086, now known as the Domesday Book, there were 87 royal burgesses holding property direct from the king, as well as 219 holding theirs from other lords, so the town was already large and had its own reeve and bailiffs.

In 1202, Northampton was one of eleven towns which purchased the right to buy and sell dyed cloth, and by the fourteenth century had a national reputation for fulling and dying with 300 cloth workers.

Northampton soon became a major trading centre for corn and horses, wool, cloth, and the dyeing of wool and cloth. Much of this is reflected in street names that remain today such as Woolmonger Street, Scarletwell Street, Marefare, Mercers Row and Horsemarket.

The town held annually one of the only four international fairs in England, not only attracting Royal buyers, but buyers and sellers from across Europe. The first reference to these fairs is to one which was held around 1180 on All Saints' Day in All Saints' Church and churchyard. In 1235 the fair moved to a waste area north of the church. This waste area became the present Market Square. There was also an annual fair held at Boughton Green just outside the town, and famed throughout England for its horses, brooms and wooden-ware. Its last day was given over to wrestling and other forms of sport. The town was also a major religious centre based around the enormous Cluniac Abbey of St. Andrew's which covered much of the area known as Semilong today. Between 1338 and 1498, 39 of 40 of the general chapters of the Benedictines were held in the Abbey despite it being Cluniac. In addition there was an Augustinian Abbey, Cluniac Priory and Nunnery, Dominican, Franciscan, Carmelite, and Austin Friars houses, as well as eight churches.

Probably because it was a religious centre, the town also became home to one of England's two fledgling universities known as studiums, the other being Oxford. It was on par with the European universities and both Geoffrey de Vinsauf, a leading proponent of the early medieval grammarian movement, and Daniel of Morley, an English scholastic philosopher and astronomer, taught there. It was during the reign of Richard I that the students migrated to Oxford, only to return to Northampton during the reign of Henry III at the time of the 2nd Barons' War. However, after the 1264 battle, Henry III forever banned a university in the town and it has only been in recent years that one has returned.

In 1215 King John authorised the appointment of William Tilly as the town's first mayor. He also ordered that 'twelve of the better and more discreet' residents of the town should join him as a council to assist in the running of the town. The importance of Northampton at this time is underlined by the fact that London, York and King's Lynn were the only other towns in England which had mayors by this date.

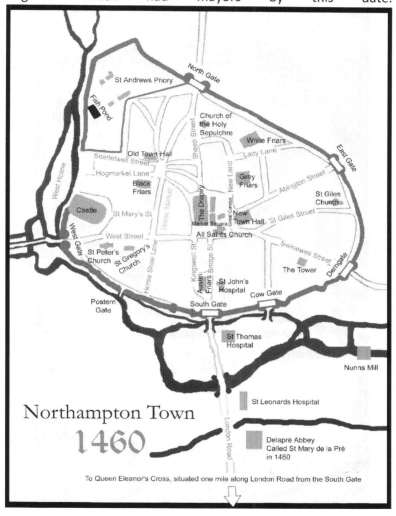

Map of Northampton in 1460 (Matthew Ryan)

The town also had the earliest and most important tournament ground outside London, where knights, their servants and onlookers gathered in their hundreds from all over Europe. Its exact location is now lost, except it was outside the town walls. It may have been either on Harlestone Heath, where the town had one of, if not the first, horse racing track in England in the early 1600s, or the modern racecourse.

Northampton's castle was one of the most important in England. It was probably originally of a motte and bailey construction, started by Simon de Senlis around 1086, and rebuilt in stone over the next two centuries. It was taken over by the King in 1130, and from then on was used as a royal residence. Sadly, there is now nothing to see as it was slighted in 1662 by the newly-restored Charles II and its substantial remains demolished when the railway station was built across its site in 1879.

With its royal castle and the town itself surrounded by a wall wide enough for six men to walk side by side, the town became a main stopping point for royal progresses and Parliaments until the reign of Richard II, and many important events in this country's history took place within its walls. It was here that the nobles swore first allegiance to Empress Matilda, King John and King Edward II. King John was excommunicated in the castle and the Parliament that led to the Peasants' Revolt took place in the town too.

Because of its strategic location, it is not surprising that the town was the site of a number of sieges and battles. The earliest medieval battle known was in 1088 during William Rufus' reign between men of the county and those of Leicester. In 1174, during the rebellion against King Henry II by his sons, the town was assaulted and 200 townsmen were killed. The county itself was central to the whole Magna Carta story, as when the Barons met at Stamford in 1215, they marched to Northampton to meet King John, but when he did not show, moved onto Brackley. It was from here that they sent John a list of demands that became the Magna Carta. When John refused their demands, they renounced their fealty and laid siege to Northampton for two weeks. From there they advanced on London and John agreed to seal the Magna Carta on 15 June 1215 at Runnymede. The Barons left the town and the townspeople attacked the castle, but were repelled. In revenge, the garrison burned down part of the town. The barons returned later that year, but the siege was broken by one of John's mercenary armies. The town was also the location for the opening battle of the 'Second Barons' War' (1264).

When Edward I's Queen, Eleanor of Castile died in 1290 at Harby, near the city of Lincoln, her body was taken back to London. Between 1291 and 1294, crosses were erected at each of the places where her funeral procession stopped overnight. Of the three surviving crosses, Northamptonshire is fortunate to have two, one being at Geddington, the other at Northampton, standing on the high ground close to Hardingstone village and above Delapré Abbey and the town.

When Richard II presided over the last Parliament to be held in the town in 1380 Richard stayed in the nearby village of Moulton. The Parliament itself was held in All Saint's church rather than the castle. It was this Parliament that led to the Peasants Revolt the following year, So, by the time of the Wars of the Roses, both the castle and the walls were in a poor state of repair.

In later times, the town would go on to play a major part in the English Civil War. The Parliamentarian army would assemble in town for their first major battle, which took place just over the county border at Edgehill on 23rd October 1642, and again for the last major and decisive battle – Naseby on 14 June 1645. In between the two, the county was split between the two sides and many, sometimes large; skirmishes took place such as those at Middleton Cheney and Wootton in 1643.

Very little of old Northampton remains today. Apart from the times it was burned down during fighting, it suffered two major fires, one in 1516 and another in 1675. Both destroyed much of the town. The expansion of the Town in the 19th century and, particularly, the coming of the railway decimated most of the surviving fabric of Medieval and Tudor Northampton.

Northampton's Queen Eleanor Cross,
Now as at the time of the battle,
headless (Author's collection)

The Wars of the Roses

The title 'Wars of the Roses' is a comparatively modern one. The idea of two noble houses with roses as their badge was first used in 1646 when Sir John Oglander published a pamphlet entitled 'The Quarrel of the Warring Roses.' In reality, only the Yorkists used a rose as their badge, the Lancastrians preferring Henry's swan badge. The red rose was probably a badge of the Beaufort family, and was not used by a king until Henry VII.

What is now known as the '*Wars of the Roses*' was in reality a series of interconnected rebellions that spanned 37 years with sixteen major battles, starting with the first battle of St. Albans in 1455, and ending with Stoke in 1487.

In this time there were four kings, 10 Coups d'états and five usurpations of the throne. There were also fifteen invasions, of which five were successful. On top of this, there were a large number of small rebellions, most of which were either stopped or failed before they started, and several private battles between warring nobles.

There were many reasons for the start of the war. When Henry V died in 1422, he was succeeded by his nine month old son who was crowned King Henry VI. The new child King also succeeded to the French throne on the death of his grandfather Charles VI, King of France, shortly afterwards. Henry inherited a long running conflict in France, known as the Hundred Years' War, where Charles VII contested his claim to the French throne. Henry married Charles' niece, Margaret of Anjou in 1445, partially in the hope of achieving peace. When the war with

France started again, the French took the upper hand and by 1453, Calais was Henry's only remaining territory on the continent. In England, great magnates with private armies dominated the countryside and lawlessness was rife. In 1450 the commons launched a rebellion against misrule, now known as *"Jack Cade's Rebellion"*. It was ruthlessly crushed with a "harvest of heads". Two years later Richard of York led another rebellion but he was forced to surrender near Dartford and placed under house arrest. Henry later proved to be feckless and simpleminded, subject to spells of madness, and totally dominated by his ambitious queen, Margaret of Anjou.

Henry lapsed into a catatonic state in 1453 and Richard, Duke of York was made Protector of the Realm. When Henry recovered at Christmas 1454, Henry's authority was re-established under Queen Margaret and her supporters, especially Edmund Beaufort, 2nd Duke of Somerset, forcing York to take up arms for self-protection. The first battle of the wars, fought in the streets of St. Albans (May 22, 1455), resulted in a Yorkist victory and four years of uneasy peace followed.

Whatever title they are given and whichever starting date is preferred, the *'Wars of the Roses'* can, however, be divided into four distinct phases:-

1450-9. Descent into War (Starting with Jack Cade's Rebellion)
1460-5. The war of succession
1469-71. The Neville rebellions and the return of the Lancastrians

1483-7. Richard III and the invasion of Henry Tudor

The Lancastrians

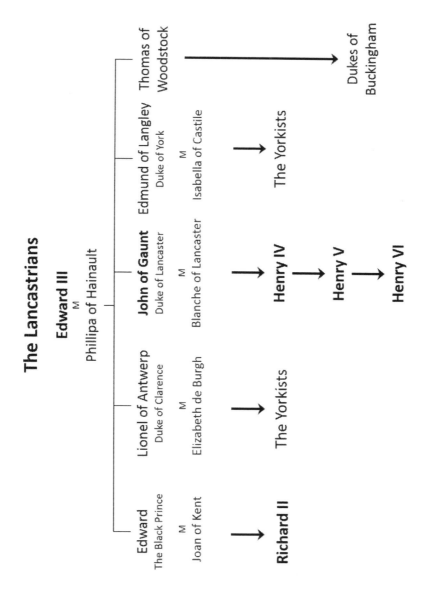

Edward III
M
Phillipa of Hainault

Edward
The Black Prince
M
Joan of Kent

→ **Richard II**

Lionel of Antwerp
Duke of Clarence
M
Elizabeth de Burgh

→ The Yorkists

John of Gaunt
Duke of Lancaster
M
Blanche of Lancaster

→ **Henry IV** → **Henry V** → **Henry VI**

Edmund of Langley
Duke of York
M
Isabella of Castile

→ The Yorkists

Thomas of
Woodstock

→ Dukes of
Buckingham

The Yorkists

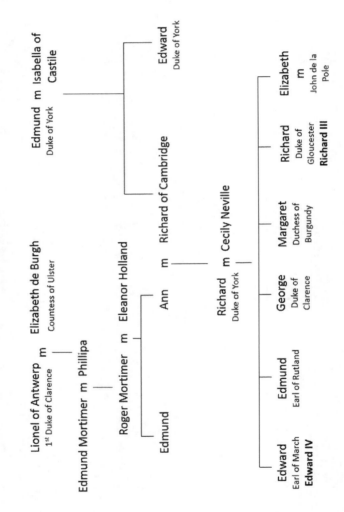

The Nevilles

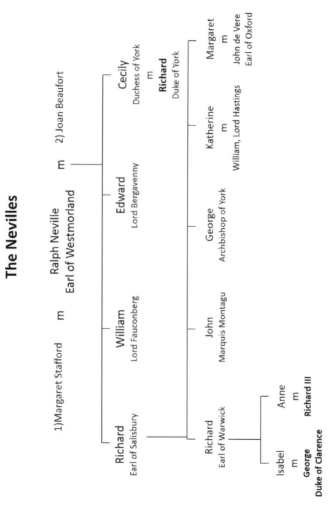

1)Margaret Stafford   m   Ralph Neville
Earl of Westmorland   m   2) Joan Beaufort

Richard
Earl of Salisbury

William
Lord Fauconberg

Edward
Lord Bergavenny

Cecily
Duchess of York
m
Richard
Duke of York

Richard
Earl of Warwick

John
Marquis Montagu

George
Archbishop of York

Katherine
m
William, Lord Hastings

Margaret
m
John de Vere
Earl of Oxford

Isabel
m
**George
Duke of Clarence**

Anne
m
Richard III

Northamptonshire at the beginning of Wars of the Roses

The county of Northamptonshire has many significant connections with the Wars of the Roses and many of the key players come from within its boundaries. At the time of the 1460 battle, Northampton was primarily under Lancastrian control. The Duke of Buckingham, who was also the Earl of Northampton, and many other nobles, including the Earl of Arundel and Richard of York, all had houses in the town; mostly in the then fashionable Swinewell Street (later renamed Derngate). Henry VI's Queen, Margaret of Anjou, had also been given the then village of Kingsthorpe as a wedding present. In March 1459 the town was also given a charter by Henry VI for its support in supressing riots and rebellions.

"Know ye that we considering not only the great and memorable services which the faithful men and Burgesses of our town of Northampton have heretofore done to us but also the great and memorable services which they have now lately performed by their daily attendance on and assistance to our royal person at their heavy costs expenses and charges for the resistance reduction and correction of divers of our rebellious people…"

It was at Fotheringhay in the north of the county that the Yorkists had their spiritual home and powerbase. It was the birthplace of the future Richard III in 1452, and his sister Margaret, who Henry VII called the diabolical duchess. Richard of York, his son Edmund (both killed at the battle of Wakefield) and wife Cecily Neville are also all buried in the church.

In May 1437, Lord Fanhope, Sir John Cornwall, who was married to Elizabeth of Lancaster, Duchess of Exeter and daughter of

John of Gaunt, began to build a new castle at Ampthill in Bedfordshire. It was less than five miles away from Reginald Lord Grey of Ruthin's principal residence of Wrest Park near Silsoe. In January 1439, violence flared between the two in Bedford when they met at a Commission of the Peace at the Shire Hall. Fanhope claimed that Grey had brought 800 men armed to the teeth, from his estates in Bedfordshire and Northamptonshire, which included Castle Ashby. In 1442, violence flared up again in Bedford and in Northampton where the common bell was rang to warn of an attack. On 6 July, the King had to send a letter commanding the burgesses of Northampton to suppress all riotous assemblies. And, on 12 July 1443, Grey was commanded to keep the peace with the people of Northampton.

At the end of April 1450, as King Henry VI was making his way to the Leicester session of Parliament, he was stopped at Stony Stratford by John Harries, a shipman from Yorkshire, wielding an agricultural flail. Harries proclaimed: "to show that the Duke of Yorke then in Yreland shuld in lyke manner fight with traytours at Leicester parliament and so thrashe them downe as he had thrashed the clods of erthe in that towne". Harries was dragged to Northampton, where he was executed as a traitor. "His hed put on the southe gate of Northamton, his quarters at Yorke, Lyncolne, Bristowe, and Oxenforde."

The Woodvilles of Grafton Regis

One family above all from the county that had an enormous impact on the Wars of the Roses was the Woodvilles (Wydeville) of Grafton Regis. They had held Grafton since the 12th century and had been High Sheriffs of Northamptonshire during the reigns of Edward III, Richard II, Henry IV, V and VI. Sir Richard

Wydeville (Woodville), was considered 'the handsomest man in England' and rose to become a squire of Henry V. At the Battle of Agincourt, he kept the King's lucky totem of a fox's tail tied to a lance "always within sight of the King" during the fighting, and was knighted afterwards. He became chamberlain to Henry V's brother, the Duke of Bedford. Then, after the Duke died, his son, also called Richard, married the widowed duchess, Jacquetta of Luxembourg. They had 16 children, and the oldest, Elizabeth, would go on to be Queen of England. This Richard was created Baron Rivers by Henry VI on 9 May 1448.

In 1451, Rivers was made Captain of Calais, a highly prestigious post. Four years later, after the battle of St. Albans, Rivers was replaced by Richard Neville, Earl of Warwick, who is now known to history as 'The Kingmaker'. However, Rivers refused to give it up and it was not until April 1456 that Warwick was finally allowed into Calais. The feud between Warwick and Rivers grew, and in January 1458, both were summoned to appear before the Great Council at Westminster to resolve their differences. Peace did not last long as six months later Rivers was appointed to lead an enquiry into Warwick's attack on the Lubeck salt fleet. The attack was effectively an act of piracy and had severely damaged relations with the Hanseatic League. As a result Warwick was replaced as Captain of Calais by the 22 year old Henry Beaufort, the new Duke of Somerset.

The Treshams of Sywell

It was also the time that the Treshams, a now famous local family, first made their name. William Tresham was a lawyer from Sywell. In 1430 he was appointed as a councillor to

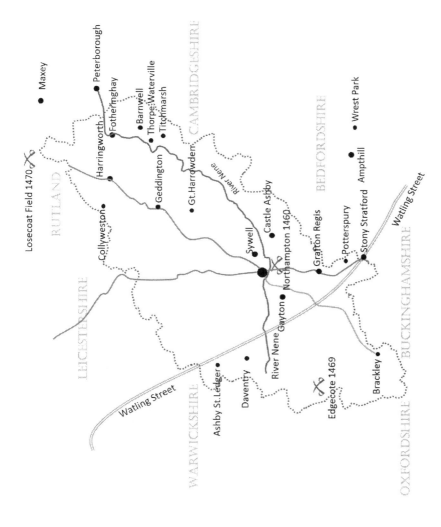

Map of Northamptonshire during the Wars of the Roses with key locations (Author)

Humphrey Stafford, Duke of Buckingham. Then in 1432 he was made one of the two Attorneys-General of Henry Beaufort, and spent much of the 1430s on various commissions of the crown. On 3 June 1442, he was appointed Chancellor of the Duchy of Lancaster and he was Speaker of the House of Commons in 1439, 1442 and 1447. In September 1450, Tresham was murdered and his son Thomas, an esquire for Henry VI, was badly wounded in Thorpland Close, Moulton, by supporters of Lord Grey of Ruthin. By 1455, Thomas was serving as an usher of the King's chamber and remained a staunch Lancastrian, taking part in the battles that followed. Other leading families include the Harringtons of Wolfage Manor (and Hornby), the Wakes of Blisworth, Greens of Boughton, Greens of Drayton, Lord Zouche of Haryngworth and Baron Vaux of Harrowden and Le Kay.

One of Northamptonshire's hidden gems, Fotheringhay Castle with its mound and with the church behind. It was here that Richard III and the 'Diabolical Duchess' was born. The church has the tombs of Richard, Duke of York, his wife Cecily Neville, and their son Edmund, as well as the second Duke of York. (Author's collection)

17

Warfare in 1460

The English are all good archers and soldiers ...
This nation is cruel and bloodthirsty and they
even fight among themselves in the same way,
waging great battles.
Gilles de Bouvier, c. 1450

Warfare in the fifteenth century followed classical Roman thought, and no self-respecting commander would be without his copy of *Vegetius' De Re Militari* (Concerning Military Matters), written in the fifth century. An updated version, *Le Livre des Faites d'Armes et de Chevalerie* (The Book of Deeds of Arms and of Chivalry) was written by Christine de Pizan in 1410 and a copy had been presented to the Queen, Margaret of Anjou by the Earl of Shrewsbury. Another version written in ballad form by an anonymous author was commissioned by Lord Beaumont and called *Knyghthode and Bataile*; it was presented to Henry VI shortly before the Battle of Northampton.

Recruitment and organisation

Before we consider the armies, weapons and warfare of the mid fifteenth century, it is necessary to look briefly at the structure of England's society in the mid fifteenth century. It was loosely divided into what was known as the three estates; those who fought, those who prayed, and those who worked. At the top was the King, and below him was the titled nobility: (in order of seniority), five Dukes, two Marquis, nine Earls and two Viscounts. These were the tenants in chief, who held huge estates throughout the country directly from the king, and considered themselves the king's natural councillors. With the final battle of the hundred year war only seven years before the battle of Northampton, a number of the nobility such as Richard, Duke of York and his wife's uncle, William Neville, Lord Fauconberg, had gained considerable experience fighting in France. Some, such as the Duke of Buckingham who had also fought in France, held more than one title and as well as Duke, was Earl of Northampton, below the nobility came around 44 barons and then the gentry. The number of gentry would have fluctuated throughout the period but, according to the 1436 tax returns, there were 183 Knights Banneret who could fight under their own banner, 750 ordinary Knights who fought under the banner of another, and below them 1,200 Esquires.

All these held their land from the tenants in chief, the bannerets typically held ten manors, lesser knights, two or three, and esquires one or two. Alongside these were 'those who prayed'. This was the church and it held considerable lands of its own. Below the nobility, gentry and church came 'those who worked'. These were mostly the tenant farmers, the servants of the nobles, and the farm labourers living in and around the nobilities, gentries and churches' manors. Since the Assize of Arms of 1181, all men were required by law to be armed according to their landholding. By 1388, it had become law that every town and village should have an archery target known as a butt and that every man between the ages of 16 and 60 should shoot arrows up and down three times every feast day. Most would start as young children on small bows, increasing the strength of the bow as they grew, so that by the time they had matured they could use a powerful warbow. They also practised fighting with other weapons, as Dominic

Mancini noted in 1483: 'it is a particular delight of this race that on holidays, their youths should fight up and down the streets clashing on their shields with blunted swords or stout staves in place of swords'.

These men, with massive upper body strength from working in the fields and archery practice since childhood, meant that there was a large pool of fighting-fit men that the nobles could call on. Also, since the collapse of the English in France seven years earlier, there would have been a pool of unemployed experienced soldiers that could have been drawn upon. No wonder that Mancini recorded that 'their bodies are stronger than other peoples' for they seem to have hands and arms of iron'.

By the fifteenth century it was common to have a document drawn up that detailed an individual's military and civil obligations to his lord in return for pay, protection, land or other benefits (often called maintenance). This document would be sealed with wax and then perforated or indented and torn in two, the lord retaining one half and the individual keeping the other. From this we get an 'indentured retainer' and a group of such men were known as a 'retinue'. A 1452 indenture between the Earl of Salisbury and one of his tenants, Sir Walter Strickland, shows that Strickland was to supply 74 billmen mounted and harnessed (wearing armour), 69 mounted archers, 76 billmen and 79 archers on foot.[1] Salisbury also brought 500 mounted retainers with him to 'Love Day' in 1458. A later example of how many men a noble could muster comes from 1483 with over 700 armed retainers from 44 different manors listed for John Howard, Duke of Norfolk.[2] Senior churchmen, such as Bishops, would also have their own retinues, although primarily for personal protection. The noble etc., would hand out clothing in his colours (called livery) and/or his badge to their men to show their allegiance to him. At Northampton, the King's men from Cheshire wore red and black with the swan badge, Buckingham's men wore black and red with the Stafford knot, Viscount John Beaumont's men wore white with his elephant badge and those of Edmund Lord Grey of Ruthin, red with the gryphon or black ragged staff badge. On the Yorkist side, Warwick's men were in red with the bear badge; Edward's men probably wore murray and blue with the falcon and fetterlock badge, but fought under his father's blue and white banner with the falcon and fetterlock, whilst Lord Fauconberg's men wore white and blue with his lion badge.

Controlling an army in the field was difficult at best, and although drums could beat time for a march or attack with trumpets sounding out commands, it was a noble's or a town's standard or banner that kept a force together. It not only identified where a particular unit was on the battlefield, but also served as rallying point, keeping men together in the confusion of a medieval battle. The most commonly depicted is the standard, which was a long tapering flag with either a rounded or swallow-tail end and showed the colours, badge, crest and motto of its owner. Its length was dependent on the status of the noble, with the king having the largest at 8–9 yards long, whilst a knight's was just 4 yards long. Some called 'Company Standards' were no more than 2 yards long and 2 feet deep, but probably more common on the battlefield was the square standard or banner, which was stiffened and had a batten along the top to keep it unfurled. These would often show a heraldic symbol or badge on the livery colours.

As well as the retinues, there was another method of recruitment. As part of the Statute of Winchester of 1285, Edward I introduced the *'commission of array'*. This was a written grant of authority from the king to appointed commissioners in towns or shires, who were normally members of the gentry, to gather all able-bodied men for military service. Notices would be pinned on church doors, but as few could read, they would be read out in town squares and in the churches. Sometime before 1468, a commission of array divided men into companies, each typically comprising between fifty and a hundred men under the leadership of a captain[3]. The town was expected to supply and pay the men whilst on the king's service within England, and twice each year royal commissioners were given authority under their commissions of array to inspect and report on the military readiness of the county or town in their charge. Once a summons had been sent out, men would frequently be expected to be ready at one day's notice. Towns would also have their own colours and badges and these would also be emblazoned on a banner. In 1455, Coventry equipped 100 archers giving them sashes of red and green, a new multi-coloured coat for its captain and a new 'Black Ram' banner. However in 1460, they only sent 40 men to Northampton. The Rose of Rouen, a poem about the Battle of Towton, lists some of the badges for other towns; for example, the 'Griffon' for Leicester, the 'Harrow' for Canterbury, the 'Wolf' for Worcester and the 'George' for Nottingham.

A third source for troops was the Calais garrison. Calais and its surrounding district (known as the Pale or Pas de Calais) with outlying castles was the last English stronghold in France and a major source of income for England through trading with the rest of Europe. The 700 or so men employed to defend it, the closest thing to a standing professional army in England, were commanded by a Captain, normally of noble birth. At the time of the battle of Northampton, this was the Duke of Somerset, although Calais was under the control of Warwick and his men who had refused to leave. The number of men in Calais at this time would have been swelled by disaffected Yorkists and their retinues.

Personal Protection

Full plate armour, or as it was called at the time, harness or cap-à-pie (head to toe), was normally a preserve of the wealthy and noble class. A complete set of plate armour made from well-tempered steel would weigh around 15–25 kg (33-55 lbs). The wearer remained highly agile and could jump, run and otherwise move freely as the weight of the armour was spread evenly throughout the body. The armour was articulated and covered a man's entire body completely from neck to toe. As a consequence it could cost as much as a high performance car today For example, in 1441 Sir John Cressy, a knight from Dodford in Northamptonshire, brought a set of Milanese armour (see below) for himself for £8 6s 8d, and another for his squire at £5 16s 8d, which totalled more than a quarter of a typical knight's annual income.[4] At the same time, an archer would have earned just 6d per day. As a consequence, very few, probably no more than 10%, would have worn full armour at

Northampton. By the 1430s two very distinct centres of armour production had emerged in Europe. The first was Italian and mainly from Milan and Brescia, with the most famous being made by the Missaglia family of Milan, now generally termed Milanese. By 1425, having discovered how to harden armour, the Italians were making considerable improvements to their designs. Smooth round surfaces, limiting where a sword might bite, and two part breastplates, with the lower one overlapping the upper one to give double the protection, became features of their armour. They also added a smaller right elbow protector (*couter*), with the upper wing larger than the lower, and a larger reinforced couter on the left arm as well as asymmetrical shoulder guards (*pauldrons*).

The second, from southern Germany, especially Augsburg, Nuremberg, Landshut, and Innsbruck, with armour made by the Helmschmied dynasty of Augsburg the most famous. In the 1420s and 1430s, their breastplate was more angular with the upper part flared out and the lower back angled into the waist, giving the armour its characteristic 'box' shape. In the 1420s a small arm defence covering the shoulder, known the *spaudler*, came into use, and by the 1450s this was attached to the upper cannon. The leg harness was very similar to that of the Italian style, although with smaller side wings on the *poleyns* and *sabatons* made of horizontal plates in the shape of contemporary footwear. However, it was not until the 1460s that it developed into a more slender, elongated form, often with fluting that we recognise today as the 'Gothic' style.

Armour was also made in England, although little survives today. There was a workshop making armour for the nobility in the Tower of London before 1450, and in 1453, Henry VI granted a charter to the London Armourers Company. This type seems to have been developed to suit fighting on foot, whereas European armour designed for mounted warfare and reinforced on the right side.

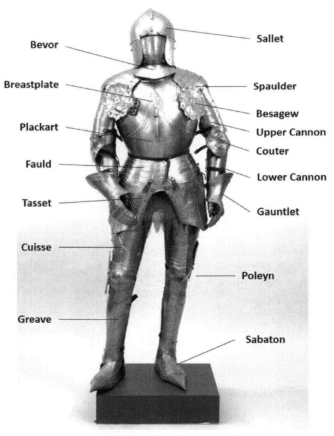

Annotated Italian suit of armour with sallet, c. 1450
(Author's collection)

Flanders and France also had their own armour industries and, among other pieces, seem to have made cheaper copies of Milanese and Gothic designs. As well as the quality armour, there were probably cheaper, massed produced and more affordable sets of armour that would not have given the same level of protection.

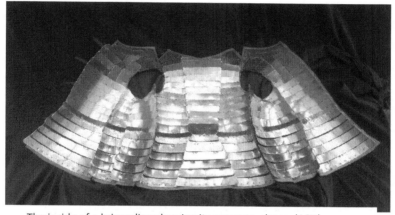
The inside of a brigandine showing its separate plates. (ASH)

Brigandines first appeared towards the end of the 14th century, and came into wide use in the 15th century. They were generally front-opening garments with small armour plates, sometimes riveted between two layers of stout cloth, or just to an outer layer, the richest being of velvet. Many brigandines appear to have had larger, somewhat 'L-shaped' plates over the central chest area. The rivets, or nails, attaching the plates to the fabric usually in threes were often gilt, or of latten, and sometimes embossed with a design. In more expensive brigandines, the outer layer of cloth was usually of velvet. Being made from small plates meant that the brigandine was far more flexible, giving a greater degree of movement than full plate and probably why it was a popular type of armour.

An arming doublet was worn beneath the armour. This was made from fustian with a velvet lining and with gussets of mail at the most vulnerable parts of the body such as the armpits. The arming doublet also had waxed cords attached called arming points, onto which the armour was attached. A mail collar and a mail skirt or pair of shorts (fauld) was also sometimes worn.

The most common helmet during the wars was called the sallet, worn by both the rich and poor, with and without full plate armour. It was a close fitting helmet with a 'tail' at the rear covering the neck. The front was cut out around the face and closed with a visor, fastened to the sides of the helmet, which could then be lifted to provide extra ventilation. A slit between the top of the visor and the helmet bowl provided vision when the visor was down. The German sallet also had a long tail over the neck, but sometimes formed of several plates, and a deep skull fitted to the shape of the head. It either had either a visor pivoted at the sides, the eye slot formed between the lower edge of the skull and the upper edge of the visor, or was in one piece with eye slots cut in the front. The first references to the sallet in Italian sources date to 1407, although it was not popular until after 1430. The German sallet seems to have first appeared in the 1420s, but seems to have been rare until the 1460s.

The Coventry sallet dating from 1460. (Herbert Art Gallery and Museum, Coventry [CC BY-SA 3.0 (http://creativecommons.org/licenses/by-sa/3.0)] via Wikimedia Common)

By the mid-fifteenth century, a regional variety of sallet had evolved in England and the Netherlands, termed the 'English-Burgundian style'. It was usually worn with a bevor (a plate gorget that extended over the chin) and had very similar facial protection and frontal appearance as the German sallet. However, it was more curvaceous and possessed a less extreme projection to the rear. French sallets were very similar to the English-Burgundian type and all have been classed as 'short-tailed sallets'. Another variation on the sallet is what is now known as an archer's sallet and frequently seen in contemporary art. This was a single piece, close fitting helmet without face protection, in a number of styles from a simple skull cap, to having either a rounded or short tailed back. An Italian equivalent was the barbute, which closely resembled classical Greek helmets. It is not clear how much they were worn in England, although John Paston enquired about a set of armour from Bruges, including a barbute in 1473.

The armet was another type of helmet, but its use seems to have been restricted to men-at-arms. The earliest surviving example dates to 1420 and made in Milan, but appears to have not become common until the end of the century and into the next. The typical armet consisted of four pieces: the skull, the two large hinged cheek-pieces which locked at the front over the chin, and a visor which had a double pivot, one either side of the skull. The cheek-pieces opened laterally; when closed they overlapped at the chin, fastening by means of a spring-pin which engaged in a corresponding hole, or by a swivel-hook and pierced staple. A multi-part reinforcement for the bottom half of the face, known as a wrapper, was sometimes added, its straps were protected by a metal disc at the base of the skull piece called a rondel.

We can get an idea of armour of a wealthy knight at the time of Northampton from the will of Sir John Fastolf, who died on 5 November 1459. In his inventory Falstolf had; three Milanese mail shirts (haubergeon), five pairs of breast and back plates, and four brigandines, one of which was covered in red velvet. There were also a number of leg and arm defences. For head protection, Falstolf had eight sallets, two with visors and interestingly, eleven of the older style of helmets that would have not been out of place at Agincourt called bascinets, five with mail that extends to cover the throat, neck and shoulders (*aventail*).[5]

A fifteenth century great bascinet (c. 1440) with rounded skull and visor, showing the position of the wearer's head and the rotation of the visor. This is possibly the type mentioned in Falstoft's inventory. (Author's collection)

The ordinary medieval soldier would have worn his everyday clothes on campaign which usually consisted of a shirt, doublet, woollen hose and boots. Most would have also worn a padded 'jack' for protection, made from layers of canvas or linen stuffed with tow, wool, straw or even scraps of mail. They were normally fastened down the front with laces and came either with or without sleeves, which were attached to the body by cords. Mancini, writing in 1483, recounts that the softer a jack was, the greater protection it afforded. The Duke of Norfolk's accounts describe his jacks as being made from eighteen folds of white 'fustian' (a coarse cloth of wool and linen) and four folds of linen, whilst Falstolf's inventory of 1459 has jacks filled with mail and horn. We can get an idea of what some of the troops raised from commissions worn from the 1457 Bridport Muster Roll. This unique document lists 201 names (four of which are women) and of these, 119 have some form of protection and weapons. It lists 74 sallets, although some have more than one, and seven men had a sallet, but no other form of protection. Two had full sets of harness, but are likely to be of an earlier period, and another two had brigandines. The most common personal defence was the jack, with 67 being listed, two of which were worn with mail shirts. Another brought a mail shirt only. There was also one set of leg armour and one set of breast and backplate.

A reenactor wearing a heavily padded jack, as worn in 1460. For the majority of those fighting this would have been their only protection. (Authors collection)

Household and retinue troops would have been better protected than the common footman, with some wearing additional armour such as brigandines. This meant that at Northampton few men would have looked the same on the battlefield except for their livery. Very few would have worn the latest armour and some would have still worn older styles.

However, the vast majority would have worn little more than a jack and sallet.

Although the shield was no longer required by the knights and men-at-arms due to the protection given by armour, lighter troops would often carry a small, round, iron or steel shields called a 'buckler'.

Some would have a large, man-sized shield called a pavise that provided protection for archers, crossbowmen and gunners, particularly whilst reloading. Some had slits to fire through, others studded with nails to act as an obstruction when thrown on the ground. Falstolf lists several of these shields in his inventory, and the Bridport Roll lists two.

A modern reconstruction of a pavise (Author's collection)

Weapons

The sword was still the main weapon of the knight throughout the Wars of the Roses, and could vary from the short and broad 'arming swords' to the narrow and long 'hand-and-a-half sword' (bastard sword). Contemporary illustrations and effigies suggest that some carried both.

Another type of sword was the single-edged Falchion, which had a short, heavy blade with the combined weight and power of an axe, but had the versatility of a sword. They were found in two different forms from the 11th century onwards. The first one was the cleaver type, which looked very similar to a large meat cleaver, but was rare if used at all, in the fifteenth century. The second was a cusped type, characterized by a straight blade with flare-clipped or cusped tips. A variation similar to the falchion was the hanger. This was also a short, single edged short sword, but with an S-shaped cross guard that formed a simple knuckle guard to protect the hand. This type was more likely a foot soldier's or archer's sword; although on the Bridport Roll, sixty-nine swords are listed; only one is described as a hanger.

A weapon popular with the nobility and footman alike was the poll-axe. The head, mounted on a pole around six feet long, had an axe on one side and a form of hammer on the opposite side. A square section spike protruded out the top of the head. Some had iron strips called *langets* running down the shaft, others a circular iron handguard. They would be used two-handed, probably like an axe, the hammer cracking armour and locking joints, the point to stab. Ten such weapons are mentioned in the Bridport Roll, and there are many shown in the hands of the nobility and gentry in contemporary illustrations too.

The majority of ordinary footmen carried staff weapons and, if contemporary images are to be believed, the most common was the simple spear. It was also the weapon of the commoners listed in the earlier statutes. However, the most common staff weapon on the Bridport Roll was the glaive. Eleven are listed on the roll, and were a knife-like blade mounted on a six foot pole, primarily for cutting.

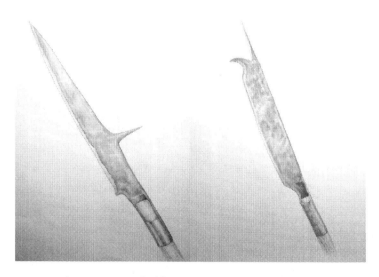

An artist's impression of a fifteenth century glaive (left) and bill (right) by Matthew Ryan, based on surviving fragments in the Royal Armouries at Leeds. (Matthew Ryan)

The bill seems to have been based on the common agricultural billhook used for chopping branches from hedges and trees. It had a pronounced forward curving blade, sometimes with a hook or spike on the back and often with a spike on top, mounted on a pole approximately 1.5–1.8m (5–6ft) long. It was a simple, practical weapon, unlike the longer, more ornate versions often seen today, which are based on guards' weapons from the time of Henry VIII.

It would have been used much in the same way in battle as it would have been used in the fields and, therefore, required no training. This is supported by contemporary European paintings which invariably show them being used over-hand. It is not clear how popular these weapons were at the time of Northampton, as only three bills were listed on the Bridport Roll. Twenty years later, the Ewlme muster roll describes most of the footmen having bills, but we do not know whether this is an actual description or generic term.

Other weapons used on the battlefield includes axes (ten are mentioned on the Bridport Roll), the lead maul (or *mass de plumbo*) and its noble equivalent, the mace. If mounted, the main weapons for the heavy cavalry was the lance and for the light cavalry - the spear. Another weapon primarily for the cavalry was the war hammer, which had a small hammer on one side and a beak on the other, mounted on a short shaft. There was also a long shafted version for fighting on foot, often referred to as the *bec-de-corbin*.

Just about everyone carried a dagger of some kind. There were three main types available in the fifteenth century, with the Rondel the most common. These were single-edged blades up to 10 inches long, with 'roundels' for the hand-guard and pommel to give a secure grip and to assist in hammering the blade home. The Ballock dagger (called a kidney dagger by the Victorians), as the name suggests, had a distinctively shaped handle, with two oval swellings at the guard resembling male genitalia and were often hung at the front. The Misericorde was similar to a stiletto and had a straight and narrow blade often triangular in section. It was frequently used to deliver a final 'mercy' blow to the mortally wounded.

The Archers

The English archer was famed throughout Europe for his skill and effectiveness in battle, and remained the backbone of armies during the Wars of the Roses. Indentures suggest a ratio of archers to footmen as 2 or 3:1, sometimes more, and in some instances, towns such as Coventry only supplied archers. Contemporary Burgundian chronicler, Phillipe de Commynes, wrote that 'in my opinion archers are the most necessary thing in the world for an army; but they should be counted in thousands, for in small numbers they are worthless'.[6] The archer's D-shaped longbow was typically made from yew, imported from Italy and Spain, and was over 1.8m (6ft) long. The string was made from flax/linen or hemp. Bows were measured by the strength it took to pull one, and if we go by the bows found on the 'Mary-Rose' the strongest could pull 81kg (180lb).

Contemporary image of archers showing a variety of
armour and helmets (Author's collection)

Between 1434 and 1436 the Calais victualler sold 1,705 bows to
soldiers, and in 1460-61 the victualler brought 380 more and
sold 147 of them to the men. Arrows were a 'cloth yard'
(around 762mm - 30in) long and made from apse (poplar) or
birch. The 'fletchings' (feathers) were made from the primary
feathers of a goose, and were 177–304mm (7–12in) long. There
were a number of different arrowheads available, although
archaeological evidence suggests the most common type in this
period was a barbed, dual-purpose arrowhead (now known as
'type 16') which was effective against most targets.

The archer would have worn either a simple skull-cap or a
close-fitting sallet with no visor, so he could pull the string back
to his cheek and take aim. There are also numerous accounts of
archers taking their boots off in battle, to get better purchase

with their feet. An archer carried 48 arrows and could shoot between twelve and fifteen arrows per minute at a range of 228m (250yd), shooting in high arcs down on to the opponents. Furthermore, once an opponent was within 90m (100yds), the archers could shoot direct into faces and weak points in armour with considerable accuracy. As well as his longbow, most archers carried some form of sword and a buckler. Of the 112 possessing bows and arrows in the Bridport Muster Roll (one has three bows, along with four staff-weapons, two jacks and two sallets), thirty-three wore a jack and sallet, with a sword and dagger or other side arm. Twenty-three of the archers also possessed various staff-weapons.

Gunpowder Weapons

It is not known with any degree of certainty when guns were first used in England, although they seem to be common by the 1320s, and the word *canonys* (cannons) first appears in England around 1378. By the fifteenth century there were many different names for cannons. The book *Knyghthode and Bataile,* which was presented to Henry VI just before the battle of Northampton, lists *crapedeaux, crapaudines, covey, courtaulds, faucons, sakers*, and *serpentines* and more than eight other types. The meaning of many of these names are now lost in time, but seem to refer to sizes and calibre (bore). When Henry marched to crush Jack Cade's rebellion in 1450, the army marched in battle order with a train of artillery that included five *"grete rebawdkins"* (multi-barrelled cannons) with four chambers, a culverin with nine chambers, a barrel of culverin powder, two serpentines, two hundred shot of stone and lead, along with thirty gunners, carpenters, smiths and masons.

Gregory describes Burgundian mercenaries at St. Albans in February 1461, having three barrelled *rebawdkins* that simultaneously fired pellets, wild-fire and arrows around 45 inches long with mighty iron heads, three feathers in the middle and another three at the end. These were fired through shutters in Pavises.

Most guns of this period were made from around ten wrought-iron bars arranged in a circle and held in place and strengthened by iron hoops. With this type, the powder was breach-loaded, with a separate chamber into which the powder was loaded. The chambers were sealed with a wooden plug,

Modern reconstruction of a rebawdkin. (Author's collection)

preventing the powder from separating, and then positioned at the back of the barrel. To ensure a good seal, a wooden wedge was hammered in behind the chamber. They were cumbersome and difficult to use, but in the mid-fifteenth century there seems to have been a revolution in their design and use. Firstly, with the invention of the wheeled carriage, the cannons were made much more portable; secondly, improvements made to black powder allowed for a greater calibre of cannonball and range of fire. Black powder was a mixture of saltpetre, sulphur and charcoal. The saltpetre was originally imported from India via Venice but, by the time of Northampton, may have been made in England as well. Sulphur was also imported, coming from two sources in medieval Europe – Sicily and Iceland. The fine, powdered mixture was confusingly known as 'serpentine powder' and was unreliable due to high water absorption of the saltpetre. How much was mixed in England and how much was imported already mixed is not known, although there was a 'powder house' at the Tower of London in 1461. Medieval guns took great skill to load: if the powder was rammed in too tight, it would not explode and too loose, it would just belch and the ball would roll out of the barrel; if the mix was wrong, it would produce coloured smoke, fizzle and bang without firing, or even explode, killing or maiming the crew. Gunpowder would not travel well either, as its constituent parts would separate if shaken, forcing it to be mixed again before use. However, in the 1420s a new process called 'corning' was developed; the powder was first made into a paste (often with the urine of a wine drinker) and then dried into balls or loaves which were then ground to a powder. This not only made it more stable, but far more powerful. It also meant different types of powder (sorted by grain size and by the ratio of its constituents) could be produced for different types of weapons. Corned powder may have been regarded as a 'black art', so it is not known how much either side would have had at Northampton, and with the death of John Judde, the Lancastrian Master of Ordinance, just two weeks before the battle, may have lost the skill to make it.

Cannons fired cast-lead balls at this time and the softer metal would deform to the shape of the barrel. However, when the cannon was fired, the wooden plug would also burst out, flattening the back of the ball, which over the next few decades necessitated an iron cube being cast into the ball to limit the deformation. It must be remembered that medieval cannonballs did not explode, instead relying on their energy to smash through enemy lines. Recent experiments with a 60mm lead ball have shown that with a flat trajectory (no elevation) they first impacted the ground at around 100m (109yds), before bouncing up to ten times to a distance of 800m (874yds). However, these tests were in ideal conditions, i.e. on flat, dry ground. At Northampton, much of the ground was soggy from the rain which would have absorbed some, if not all, of their energy.

A modern reconstruction of a medieval cannon, showing the breach. (Author's collection)

41

We do not know to what extent handguns were used at Northampton. As early as 1411, John the Fearless, Duke of Burgundy, could field 4,000 handgunners, and both Warwick at the Second Battle of St. Albans, eight months after Northampton, and Edward IV, when he entered London in 1471, seem to have preferred mercenaries from the Low-countries. Although no record of them is known, some may have even come over from Calais with Warwick in 1460. It is not until 1467 that the Calais garrison began to purchase their own handgunnes.[7]

The earliest type of *handgonne* consisted of a short round, hexagonal, or octagonal bronze or iron barrel mounted on a much longer wooden pole. Johann Hartlieb in his 1411 "*Kriegbuch*" shows pole mounted *handgonnes*. They were called a *harquebus*, or a *hakenbüchse* in Germany, *hackbut* by the English and *arquebus* by the French. These had a simple S-shaped trigger, called a serpentine, which fastened to the side of the gun stock. This pivoted in the middle and had a set of adjustable jaws, or '*dogs*', on the upper end which held the smouldering end of a length of match that had been soaked in saltpetre. Pulling up on the bottom of the serpentine brought the tip of the match down into contact with powder in the '*flashpan*', a small, saucer-shaped touch-hole.

After 1440, aiming from the cheek, over the shoulder, or with a shortened stock propped against the shoulder, became popular. Gun makers realised that a heavier, shorter stock was as effective at absorbing recoil, but arms for use in fortifications still retained their characteristic hook on the barrel. Around this time, barrels also lengthened to between 500 and 1000mm (20-

40 inches), and the calibre dropped to between 12.5 and 16 mm. At least two surviving guns, found at Tannenburg and Morko, if correctly dated to before 1460, are of small calibre, and balls of these small calibres were found on the eastern side of Northampton battlefield in 2015, quite possibly come from such weapons.

Logistics and the army on the march

An army would typically march 15 miles per day, although Edward IV, *en-route* to Tewkesbury in May 1471, force marched his men 35 miles in one day. Men were expected to carry their own weapons, equipment and supplies with them. Some, especially the men-at-arms, would have carried their equipment in carts. A treatise written around 1450, known as the Hastings MS, lists what each man-at-arms should take in the field and included; a tent, a chair, a basin, a board and a pair of trestles to set his meat and drink on, a board cloth, a knife for cutting his meat, a cup to drink from, and a hammer and nails. Recommended food includes six loaves of bread, two gallons of wine and a mess of meaty flesh or fish.

Although a man was expected to carry his own food with him on the march, it was likely that it would soon run out. *Knyghthode and Bataile* warns of the importance of adequate supplies when its author wrote:

> *Have purveyance of forage and victual*
> *For man and horse; for iron smiteth not*
> *So sore as hunger doth if food fail.*

Writing in 1498, Venetian envoy Andrea Trevisan said *"that when war is raging most furiously, they [the English] will seek for good eating, and all their other comforts, without thinking of what might befall them"*. Therefore, a good supply of food was essential in maintaining the morale and fighting capacity of the army. The king or commander of the army would be expected to pay for what supplies were needed, although this did not always happen in practice, and occasionally towns were expected to hand over supplies free of charge. Sir John Fortescue wrote around the time of Northampton that:

"And for that his highness nor his said company in no wise should be destitute or wanting of victuals for man or horse: He strictly chargeth and commandeth every victualler, and all other his subjects dwelling in every town or place where his said highness and his said company shall come, to provide and make ready plenty of bread and ale, and other victuals, as well for horse as for man, at reasonable price in ready money therefor to them".[8]

Victuallers would therefore normally ride ahead and secure what supplies they could; harbingers would look for billets and sites to make camps and foragers would also be sent out for extra supplies and fodder. *Knyghthode and Bataile* describes the role of the harbinger as:

A Mesurer, that is our Herbagere,
For pavilion and tent assigneth he
The ground, and saith 'Be ye there, be ye here!'
Each hostel eek, in castle and city,
Assigneth he, each after a degree.

However, Gregory writes that it was a matter of contention that the mounted infantry would ride ahead and take all the best billets, then eat and drink all the supplies before the footmen arrived.

As well as the men and food supplies, an army needed to take huge supplies of arrows and equipment, such as bridges. They also took all the associated trades needed to maintain them in the field, such as blacksmiths, coopers, farriers, carpenters, masons, arrow makers etc., and all their equipment. Both sides brought cannons to Northampton and we can get an idea of the size of a small artillery train from Burgundian documents relating to the transportation of five medium serpentines, four small serpentines, a bombard and two 'courtaux' from Luxembourg to Dijon in 1474.[9] Each medium serpentine needed three horses to pull it, the small ones – two. They took thirty casks of powder, five casks per cart with four horses to pull each cart. Another one and a half carts were needed for the unspecified number of lead shot, and five for the stone shot. Sixteen horses were needed to pull the two 'courtaux' and five carts for 200 stone shot for them. Another twenty-four horses were required to pull the bombard with ten carts to carry its mantlet and ten carts to carry the one hundred stone shot taken for it. They also took 2,500 bows, 2,700 arrows and 6,000 strings in eleven carts. Four carts were needed for the saddler, cooper, carpenters and tools, two carts were needed for the gunners and their equipment. So, in total, this train alone needed 50 carts and 257 horses, just for twelve guns.[10]

An army on the march could therefore be of considerable length and as much as one day's march from one end to the other, and that is without the women, tradesmen etc., that would inevitably follow the army. *Knyghthode and Bataile* warns of how cumbersome moving three divisions as one body was, saying it was preferable to take a smaller one. It was, therefore, not uncommon for armies to march in separate battles along different routes, as Warwick and Fauconberg did at Northampton. Even then, the mounted troops had to stop to wait for the slower moving parts to catch up.

Light horse, referred to as *scourers*, *aforeriders* or *prickers*, protected the flanks of the slower moving infantry and baggage on the march. There were also behind-riders, which were light cavalry and archers to protect the rear.[11] Identifying the enemy and its movements was as critical then as it is today. Both sides would have used scourers as the medieval equivalent of scouts. However, their skills left a lot to be desired, and at the time of Blore Heath, Somerset's and Warwick's armies passed within a few miles of each other without spotting the other. Warwick's scourers also failed to detect the Queen's army as it descended on St. Albans in 1461.

Tactics

An army would normally be divided into three divisions or '*battles*' called the *vanward* or *vanguard* (sometimes just the van), the *mainward* or *mainguard* and the rearward or *rearguard*. The terms can be somewhat deceiving as the vanward could mean either the front or right-hand battle; it could also mean the division with the best troops. Similarly, the *mainward* could be the centre battle and rearward the left-hand battle. Each division would be commanded by one or two nobles. A letter from George Neville to Francesco Coppini, the papal legate, written after the Battle of Towton, describes their role:

"I prefer you should learn from others than myself how manfully our King [Edward IV], the Duke of Norfolk, and my brother and uncle bore themselves in this battle, first fighting like common soldiers, then commanding, encouraging and rallying their squadrons like the greatest captains."[12]

Both sides normally fought on foot, a tradition dating back to the Hundred Years War and battles such as Crecy (1346), Poitiers (1356), and Agincourt (1415). Commynes notes that in all of his nine battles, Edward IV fought on foot and Mancini, writing in 1483, commented that:

"Not that they are accustomed to fighting from horseback, but because they use horses to carry them to the scene of engagement, so as to arrive fresher and not tired by the fatigue of the journey; therefore they will ride any sort of horse, even pack horses. On reaching the field of battle the horses are abandoned, they all fight together under the same conditions so that no one should retain any hope of fleeing."[13]

The battle of Northampton was only the third time Englishman had fought Englishman since the battle of Shrewsbury in 1405. The first was St. Albans in 1455, and was a street fight although judging by accounts, the archers still dominated the fighting; at the second at Blore Heath, just nine months before Northampton, the Lancastrian cavalry commanded by Lord Audley charged the dismounted Yorkist's lines and were destroyed. It was followed by assault by 4,000 foot, who met a similar fate.

With so many archers on both sides during the Wars of the Roses, the tactical supremacy of the archer was somewhat negated, however, to leave them behind could have devastating consequences, as the Welsh discovered at the Battle of Edgecote. Here, separated from their archers, the Welsh infantry had to endure a relentless hail of arrows, with no way of replying. They were forced to charge the rebel army and were cut to pieces. Archers could be placed either with their 'battles' or as at Bosworth, in a long line at the front of the army. After the initial archery duel, or once the arrows ran out, the archers would revert to their light infantry role and fight with sword and buckler or other side arms. At the end of the day, all battles would have to be decided by 'hand-strokes' rather than the arrow. Both sides, therefore, looked elsewhere for tactical advantages.

Field Fortifications

Fortified field works had become a feature of warfare towards the end of the Hundred Years War and the beginnings of the Wars of the Roses. In February 1452, during York's first rebellion, his army marched to Dartford and set up a fortified camp on common land known as Sandhill on Brent heath, between Dartford and Crayford, with one side against the river Darent. By this time it was estimated that York had with him 20,000 men, including 6,000 under Devon and another 6,000 under Cobham. The most detailed account of the camp comes from Cottonian Roll, ii. 23, which says that the camp was defended by 3,000 guns with York in the centre; Cobham on the water side and Devon on the northern side. Seven ships were also anchored nearby, loaded with all the men's baggage. Benet's Chronicle on the other hand, only described the camp as being strongly fortified for his own defence, with posts, ditches and guns. However, it was not put to the test as York was tricked into surrendering before any fighting took place. In July 1453, the French built a fortified camp armed with 300 guns at Castillon. This consisted of a deep trench with a wall of earth behind it, which was strengthened by tree-trunks and a palisade on three sides, and a steep bank of the River Lidoire on the fourth. The defences were also built in an irregular, wavy line, which enabled the guns to enfilade any attackers. This time, the Anglo-Gascon cavalry, under the Earl of Shrewsbury, was destroyed trying to take it. Then, in October 1459, York built a fortified camp outside Ludlow at Ludford Bridge. It was noted that his men made a great deep ditch and fortified it with guns, carts and stakes. However, when the Calais garrison went over the Lancastrians, the Yorkists retreated and so, once again, the defences were not tested.[14] Banks and ditches were not the only type field defences, as Gregory noted at St. Albans in February 1461. He wrote that Warwick's men had nets of cord, 24 feet long and four foot wide with an upright nail through every knot and many caltrops - star shaped spikes, that always landed with one point facing upwards.[15] But, the failure of the defences to protect the Lancastrians at Northampton (and possibly, the failure of the guns), meant that a field fortification was never used again during the Wars of the Roses. They would, however, continue to be used on the continent into the next century.

The Rout

Battle would normally continue until one side broke and ran from the field. It was at this point that the rout - the systematic hunting down of the fleeing, panicking men began. Men would be hunted down, killed and stripped of all their armour and valuables. Weighed down by armour, the nobles and gentry were the prime targets. After the second battle of St. Albans, Whethamstede, a probable eye-witness, wrote that Warwick's army *"... turned their backs on the northern men and fled. And the northern men seeing this pursued them very swiftly on horseback; and catching a good many of them, ran them through with their lances"*.[16]

It was particularly nasty for battles fought near rivers such as Northampton, Wakefield, Towton and Tewkesbury. Many would also drown trying to cross the river to escape the carnage. Others, trapped by the watercourse, would be cut down where they stood. The description of the rout after Tewkesbury in May 1471, is very similar to what probably happened at Northampton:

"[The Duke of Somerset's men]... took flight in the park, and into the meadow that was near, and into the lanes and dykes where they best hoped to escape the danger. Never the less, many were distressed, taken and slain... And so it befell in the chase that many of them were slain, and at the mill, in the meadow by the town, many of them drowned. Many ran towards the town, many to the church, to the abbey, and elsewhere, as best they might."[17]

There would be little mercy for those who were caught. In August 1996, workmen discovered a grave pit from the Battle of Towton, which measured 6m x 2m and was only 50 cm in depth. Archaeologists recovered from the pit the almost complete remains of 43 individuals. Most had horrific head wounds, many to the top and back of the head, suggesting that they were caused during the rout. One of them had taken a cut that had almost sliced his jaw off in a previous battle but had recovered sufficiently to fight again.

The rout, by its nature, could cover a large area, even if the site of the battle was small. George Neville's letter to Coppini in the aftermath of Towton, remarked that immediate burial of the dead from the battle may have not been possible because they were spread over a huge area, six miles long, and almost four miles wide.[18]

A reenactor carrying a poll-axe, a popular weapon for both the nobility and peasants. (Author's collection)

To War

"men ought either to be well treated or crushed, because they can avenge themselves of lighter injuries, of more serious ones they cannot; therefore the injury that is to be done to a man ought to be of such a kind that one does not stand in fear of revenge".

Niccolo Machiavelli, *The Prince*. 1513

During the summer of 1459, tensions between King Henry VI, Queen Margaret of Anjou and their court on one side and Richard, Duke of York and his allies on the other had reached crisis point. According to An English Chronicle, a great council was held at Coventry. Richard, Duke of York, who was at Ludlow, his father-in-law Richard Neville, Earl of Salisbury, who was at Middleham and his son Richard, Earl of Warwick, who was in Calais and who would later become famous as the Kingmaker, was not invited.

Other nobles excluded were the Earl of Arundel, York's brother-in-law Viscount Henry Bouchier, and his brother Thomas, the Archbishop of Canterbury, as well as the Bishops of Ely and Exeter. In other words, York's allies; by this time, the Queen *"ruled the realm as she liked"*[19] and in the council meeting declared the Yorkists, as they were known, traitors, claiming they 'planned to come in arms to Kenilworth and take the King by surprise'[20].

On hearing the news of the council meeting, the Yorkists, fearing the worst, began to assemble an army at Ludlow. In the meantime, the Lancastrians began to assemble their army at

Nottingham. Warwick made his way from Calais, bringing with him troops from its garrison under Anthony Trollope, who had formerly been a pirate in the English Channel and a supporter of the Duke of Somerset. Salisbury, *en-route* to Ludlow, was intercepted by a large Lancastrian contingent under Lord Audley at Blore Heath on 23 September 1459. The Lancastrian army was totally destroyed, as first their cavalry, then infantry threw themselves onto Salisbury's lines.

From Ludlow, the Yorkists advanced to Worcester, where in a solemn ceremony at the cathedral, they bound themselves by faith to aid and succour one another. In a letter to the King they protested their loyalty and their intent to the prosperity and augmentation of the common weal of the realm.[21]

The King replied by offering a pardon to York and Warwick (but not Salisbury), if they surrendered within six days. But the King, or more likely the Queen, was making plans to complete the Yorkists downfall, summoning Parliament to meet at Coventry in December. Faced with an army twice the size, the Yorkists fell back to Ludlow. The King and his army followed.

The Parliament of Devils

When the Yorkists reached Ludlow on 12 October 1459, they camped on the south side of the River Teme, close to Ludford Bridge, fortifying it with carts and guns. That evening, not wishing to commit treason, Trollope, along with the majority of the Calais garrison, crossed to the King's side. According to the contemporary Burgundian chronicler, Jean de Wavrin, this was after Trollope received a message from the Duke of Somerset, his old commander.[22]

The Yorkist leadership fled, leaving their army with standards and banners flying. York and his second son, Edmund, headed to Ireland, whilst his seventeen year old son, Edward, Earl of March, along with Salisbury and Warwick fled to the safe haven of Calais via Guernsey. The Lancastrians sacked the town of Ludlow and drunk on looted wine, committed many outrages.

On 20 November 1459, the promised Parliament opened in the chapter house of St. Mary's priory, Coventry. With elections to the Parliament called for and controlled by the Queen and her supporters, the 260 members of the Commons were almost all Lancastrian in their sympathies. Its central business was the passing of an *Act of Attainder* against the leading Yorkists. The Act of Attainder had been developed so the faction in power could convict its political opponents of treason, condemning them to death, without bringing them to trial. By passing a Bill of Attainder, Parliament simply declared anyone named in the act to be guilty of treason and subject to the loss of all civil rights and the forfeiture to the Crown of all property. Because attainder declared anyone so convicted to be *"corrupt of blood,"* all heirs and descendants of attainted persons were disinherited, thus allowing the confiscated property to be parcelled out amongst supporters of the King and Queen.

It was in this Parliament that two Northamptonshire men took centre stage. Committed Lancastrian Thomas Tresham was elected Speaker of the Commons, and Thomas Thorpe, who drew up the act of attainder against the Yorkists. Thorpe had been in possession of Barnwell manor in Northamptonshire and its magnificent castle, described as *'the first example in Britain of the most monumental type of castle architecture'* since 1447.[23] He also was tenant-in-chief of Lilford in Northamptonshire and several manors in Essex. His parliamentary career began in October 1449 when he was elected to Parliament as a junior knight of the shire of Northamptonshire with Thomas Tresham. He was later knight of the shire for Essex and was elected Speaker for the first part of the 19th Parliament of King Henry VI in 1453. The following year he was imprisoned in the Fleet Prison for falsely confiscating property of the Duke of York and was replaced as Speaker by Sir Thomas Charlton. In 1455, he became Chancellor of the Exchequer, but his enemy, the Duke of York, accused him of intercepting messages to the King which might have prevented the Battle of St. Albans, and Thorpe was stripped of all his public offices.

Parliament opened with a speech by the Chancellor, William Waynflete, Bishop of Winchester, preaching on the text *'Grace to you and peace be multiplied'*. The bill accused twenty-four persons, including York, his two eldest sons and the Nevilles of levying war against the King at Blore Heath and Ludford, and three more including the countess of Salisbury of plotting his death elsewhere. It listed York's treasons since 1450; the battle at St. Albans in 1455, which was described as an *'execrabill and moost detestable dede'*, prompted by *'the moost diabolique unkyndnesse and wrecched envye'*. At the end of the session, Henry VI mitigated the effects of the act, insisting on a proviso that he could grant full pardon and restoration to those who humbly sought his grace. On 11 December 1459, the assembled

66 members of the Lords took an oath of loyalty to the King and, more importantly, his son. Parliament was dissolved nine days later, in time for Christmas. It would be known to posterity as *'The Parliament of Devils'*.

Countdown to War

The Irish welcomed York, who had fled there after the confrontation at Ludford. On 4 December 1459, Henry appointed the Earl of Wiltshire as Lieutenant of Ireland, although he did little to take up his post. However, Yorkist sources claim that Wiltshire wrote to the native chiefs encouraging them to drive the Yorkists out. It was the Yorkists in Calais that were more of a problem as this was England's gateway to Europe. In November, Henry Beaufort, the Duke of Somerset, son of the Duke who was killed by Yorkists at St. Albans in 1455 was appointed Captain of Calais and sent with a fleet to prise Warwick and the Yorkists out. His force included Lords Thomas Roos (Ros) of Rockingham, Andrew Trollope and the men who changed sides at Ludford. However, it was a disaster for the Lancastrian cause. When his fleet reached the harbour they were greeted by cannon fire and driven off. Some crews defected and others, who were blown into the port by the wind, captured. Those caught who had previously defected at Ludford were promptly executed. Lord Roos sailed on to Flanders, but Somerset and the remains of his fleet sailed a few miles west to the fortress of Guisnes and, on a promise to pay its garrison pay owed to them, were allowed access. From here, Somerset launched repeated raids against Calais, but was always beaten off.[24]

The government began to prepare a relief force at Sandwich to go to Somerset's aid, under the command of Lord Scales and the Woodvilles. They were ready to sail by early January, but in the early hours of 15 January 1460, a daring raid from Calais, led by John Dynham with 800 or so men, captured a large number of ships loaded with artillery. Richard Woodville, Lord Rivers, his wife, Jacquetta, dowager Duchess of Bedford, and his son, Sir Anthony, were also captured, whilst still in their beds, and taken back to Calais in triumph.[25]

A letter from William Paston to his son John, written at the time describes how:

"...my Lord Ryvers was brougth to Caleys, and by for the Lords with viij torches, and there my Lord of Salesbury reheated[berated] hym, callyng hym knaves son, that he schuld be so rude to calle hym and these other Lords traytors, for they schall be found the Kyngs treue liege men, whan he schuld be found a traytour, etc. And my Lord of Warrewyk reheted hym, and seyd that his fader was but a squyer, and broute up with Kyng Herry the V, and sethen hymself made by maryage, and also made Lord, and that it was not his parte to have swyche langage of Lords, beyng of the Kyngs blood. And my Lord of Marche reheted hym in lyke wyse. And Sir Antony was reheted for his langage of all iij. Lords in lyke wyse..."[26]

After the attack on Sandwich, a new fleet was ordered to be assembled safely out of reach of Calais under Sir Baldwin Fulford, Sheriff of Devon, but it had still not put to sea in March when Warwick sailed to Ireland with his Gascon Admiral, Lord Duras, and 500 men to confer with York. Details of their meeting are not recorded. No doubt it included their plans to invade England and take back the lands lost during the Parliament of Devils, by force - if necessary, but, according to Wavrin, they began to discuss the unthinkable – that York would take the throne of England for himself.

Preparations

With the threat of invasion from two sides, Jasper Tudor was sent by the Queen to Wales, taking rebel held castles, such as Denbigh, by force and securing likely landing places such as Milford Haven. Potential landing places in the south of England, such as Winchelsea and Southampton, were refortified and Commissions of Array were sent throughout the country to put men on readiness for the inevitable invasion. Commissions of Oyer and Terminer also roamed the country, winkling out and arresting Yorkist supporters and sympathisers. One such commission in June 1460, led by James Butler, Earl of Wiltshire and Treasurer of England, with the Lords Scales and Hungerford, descended on the Yorkist town of Newbury. Several of its inhabitants were drawn, hanged and quartered, a number of others were imprisoned at Wallingford, and many more were heavily fined. In the weeks preceding the battle Thomas Tresham, along with Sir Edmund Hampden, Sir John Chalers, Edward Longford, John Pury and Everard Digby, all members of the royal household, had kidnapped the Yorkist, Sir Robert Harcourt, from his home in Stanton Harcourt in Oxfordshire. Harcourt later alleged that they held him prisoner for seven weeks, preventing him from joining the other Yorkists at Northampton.[27]

After spending Christmas at Leicester, the King, Queen and their court spent the early months of 1460 touring the East Midlands, including Bedford, Cambridge and St. Albans. The only places they stopped at for more than one or two days were Northampton (30 Jan – 10 Feb), and Peterborough Abbey (6-22 April). On 18 June 1460, they returned to Coventry, where they remained until the Yorkists finally landed.

As early as 1456, it was admitted that the King was *"not yet sufficiently furnished of guns, gunpowder and other habilments of war"*. A warrant appointing John Judde, a London merchant, Master of the King's ordnance, had been issued in December 1456. Judde was contracted to address this deficiency by making sixty serpentines (field guns) with twenty tons of saltpetre and sulphur for gunpowder. On 19 May the following year, he received payment for a further twenty six serpentines, a culverin and a mortar, plus all the necessary equipment and gunpowder, to be delivered to Kenilworth castle. In the same autumn, three *'great serpentines that would be able to subdue any castle or place which the rebels might try to use'* were added to the arsenal. During the autumn of 1459, Judde was instructed to seize all the armaments that belonged to York, Warwick and Salisbury, which, after the years of campaigning in France, must have amounted to a considerable number of guns. Therefore, even a conservative estimate would give them in excess of 100 field pieces to take with the army to Northampton, and still leave more at Kenilworth. Just weeks before the battle at Northampton, on 22 June 1460, Yorkist sympathisers ambushed and killed Judde *en-route* to Kenilworth, with more guns for the arsenal.

Lord Audley and Humphrey Stafford of Southwick were sent with another small force to reinforce Somerset however, storms blew them into Calais harbour and they too were taken prisoner. On 23 April 1460, Somerset launched yet another attack on Calais along the Boulogne Road. This time he was met by the garrison at Pont de Neullay (Newnham Bridge) and his dwindling army destroyed.

Warwick returned from Ireland late in May, prudently sending a fast caravel ahead of his small fleet to reconnoitre the route. The caravel discovered a large fleet waiting for them commanded by York's son-in-law Henry Holland, Duke of Exeter. With the wind behind them, Warwick's ships bore down on their would-be attackers. Exeter, expecting Warwick to run in the face of such overwhelming odds, simply turned tail and fled to safety in Dartmouth harbour.

The Queen's actions over the preceding months show that she and her Lancastrian supporters wanted nothing less than the total destruction of the Yorkist 'rebels'. Having taken away their lands and disinherited their descendants, to complete their plan they had to remove those that remained alive. The only way to do this was to finish what they had tried to do at Ludford Bridge, bring them to battle, and kill or capture both York and the Nevilles. As we have seen, their next attempt; assaulting Calais, had also ended in failure. They had no alternative now but to wait for the Yorkists to return to England.

In the meantime, the Yorkists launched a propaganda campaign worthy of any modern spin doctor. A letter of grievance was circulated throughout England from Calais (but probably composed in Ireland). It was addressed to the Archbishop of Canterbury and professed the Yorkists' loyalty to the King and stated that no harm was intended to his person. Following the pattern first established in the Magna Carta, it listed twelve complaints of misrule. The letter criticised the King (or more likely the Queen) for introducing a new system that every town should contribute men for a standing army after the French model. How far this had been put into practice is now unknown. It accused the Queen of planning to have Henry abdicate in favour of her illegitimate son, Edward. How true the accusation of illegitimacy was remains unknown. It was however, repeated many times and at the time of Edward's conception Henry appears to have been in a catatonic state. Rumours at the time pointed the finger at the Duke of Somerset, the Queen's closest supporter, as the real father. Royal ministers were accused of plotting to destroy the Duke, and the manifesto singled out the Earl of Shrewsbury, the Earl of Wiltshire and Viscount Beaumont as *"mortalle and extreme enemyes"*. It finally called on the Archbishop and the commonalty to assist them to assert their innocence and end misrule.[28]

Soon after, fearing a repeat of the sacking of Newbury, the commons of Kent sent messages to the Calais Lords asking them if *"they wolde in alle haste possible come and socour thaym fro theyre enemyes, promyttyng that they wolde assyste theym with alle thayre power"*.[29]

A rhyme was posted on the gates of Canterbury littered with biblical and religious references and included the stanza:

> *"Time has come falsehood to destroy*
> *Time to root out the weeds from the corn*
> *Time to burn the brambles that bothers trees,*
> *Time to pluck up that the false hunter with his home."[30]*

It was at this time that King Henry was presented with 'Knyghthode and Bataile' although essentially an English translation in ballad form of Vegetius' fourth century treatise on warfare, its anonymous author also attacked the Yorkists:-

> *"O gracious our Kyng! Thei fleth his face.*
> *Where ar they now? Summe are in Irelonde,*
> *In Walys other are, in myghti place,*
> *And other han Caleys with hem to stonde,*
> *Thei robbeth & they reveth see & londe;*
> *The kyng, or his ligeaunce or amytee,*
> *Thei robbe anende, and sle withoute pitee."[31]*

The Pope Takes Sides

Events then took on an international dimension when Francesco Coppini, Bishop of Turni (Turin) arrived in Calais. In January 1459, Coppini had been sent to England by the new Pope, Pius II as orator and *referendarius* with instructions to promote a crusade against the Turks, inviting Henry to send a delegation to a congress at Mantua later in the year, and to settle dissensions between the Yorkists and Lancastrians. Whethamstede described him as *"short of stature and very little, not at all distinguished in outward appearance, but vivacious in temperament and so gifted with oratorical ability."[32]*

Coppini also had a secret mission. Both the Pope and Francesco Sforza, Duke of Milan were supporting Ferdinand (Ferrante), the illegitimate son of Alfonso V the Magnanimous, King of Aragon, Valencia, Sicily and Sardinia (who had died in 1458), against Rene of Anjou, the father of Margaret of Anjou the English Queen, who had claimed the throne of Sicily and John of Calabria, her brother, who claimed the throne of Naples. Both of the Angevin candidates also had the backing of the King of France, Charles VI, and Pius and Sforza were trying to force him to withdraw his support. With Queen Margaret controlling England, it was unlikely that the Lancastrians would interfere in Franco-Italian affairs, however, a Yorkist government might. Hidden in a letter to Sforza, written in invisible ink, soon after the battle, Coppini wrote from Canterbury saying that *"If the lords here, the kinsmen of the king, who through my hands have won back the state, had some incitement they would go to France with a considerable force to vindicate the claims of this kingdom a war with France"*. It continued, if the Yorkists did invade, the French would not be able to support the house of Anjou, and Ferrante would have a better chance of securing the throne.[33]

In December 1459, Pius II promoted Coppini to Legate for all the dominions, cities, lands and places subject to Henry, King of England. But in March 1460, Coppini was in Bruges and in a letter to Francesco Sforza said he had left England on Warwick's advice, however he would be *"returning any day by the encouragement received from thence, and we have no doubt of success if we have help thence."*[34]

In the Pope's autobiography written before 1464, he recounts a report from Coppini, written soon after Warwick's return to Calais, that the Yorkists had summonsed Coppini to meet them at Calais. Coppini's report continues with a report of a scathing denunciation of the Lancastrians by Warwick:

"Our King is a dolt and a fool who is ruled instead of ruling. The royal power is in the hands of his wife and those who defile the king's chamber. Because I could not endure this state of things and desired another form of government I was banished from the king's presence... Many feel as I do chief amongst them the Duke of York, who would now be on the throne if there were any regard for justice, We shall soon have armed forces and shall put our fortunes to the test of the sword. If God gives us victory we shall drive our foes from the King's side and ourselves govern the kingdom. The King will retain only the bare name of sovereign." [35]

When Warwick had first made contact with Coppini is unclear, but it was probably on one of the many trips to Europe (probably via Calais) that Coppini had made since first arriving in England in 1459. By mid-June 1460 he was staying in Calais and on 25 June, the Yorkists drew up a set of articles addressed to him. They professed their loyalty to King Henry and the Pope and how they intended no harm to their King. However, reform of the English government was needed and they asked Coppini to mediate. [36]

The Return of the Calais Lords

The next day Fauconberg sailed for Sandwich with Sir John Wenlock and John Dynham. There they found several hundred soldiers under Osbert Mundford who was preparing yet another relief force for Somerset. After a short battle the port was taken, and a number of soldiers were captured, including Mundford who was taken to Calais' Ryebank tower and beheaded. There were few recorded casualties on the Yorkist side, although at some point during the fighting, Dynham received a gunshot wound to the leg.

With a bridgehead established, the main Yorkist force led by Warwick, Salisbury and March, along with Audley (who seems to have changed sides after his capture), and around 2,000 men landed at Sandwich the following day. They immediately set out for Canterbury where they were met outside the walls at St. Martin's church by Robert Horne, John Scot and John Fogge. These three and their men had been sent by King Henry under a Commission of Array to resist a Yorkist landing. However, instead of stopping them, they joined them and helped negotiate entry to the city. Around this time the Yorkists were also joined by Lord Cobham who had supported York in 1452 and Edward Neville, Lord Abergavenny who was named second to Buckingham in the same Commission as Horne.[37]

The Yorkists sent out letters to all the Cinque Ports asking for their assistance. Rye's mayor and bailiff sent Morris Gedard by boat to see how Winchelsea was going to respond before both ports sent men the next day. Lydd also seems to have sent men.[38] After saying mass at the shrine of St. Thomas Becket in the

Cathedral, they marched on London via Rochester and Dartford taking St. Thomas's sacred cross with them. En-route they were joined by many others and by the time they approached London, they numbered 500 mounted men and between 20,000 and 40,000 *"footmen of the commons of Kent, Sussex and Surrey"*.[39] With so many men heading towards the city, it was thrown into disarray. The pro-Henry Lord Mayor of London advocated keeping them out and some suggested setting cannon on London Bridge to stop them. However, the day before they arrived, the Common Council changed its mind and decided to allow the Lords in. On 2 July 1460, the Yorkist lords were met by William Grey, Bishop of Ely and George Neville, Bishop of Exeter (Warwick's brother), both with armed retinues in Southwark. They accompanied the Yorkist lords over London Bridge to their lodgings in Greyfriars at Newgate. It was also noted that as they crossed the bridge, thirteen men were crushed by the crowd.[40] The rest of the army waited in the fields outside Smithfield. On entering the city the Yorkist lords removed the putrefying heads of executed Yorkists from London Bridge for burial.

Those remaining loyal to the King in the city, Thomas, Lord Scales, Jean le Foix, Earl of Kendal with Lords Lovell, Hungerford, Delaware and Vescy and a number of the royal household barricaded themselves into the Tower.

At the time the Yorkists were marching on London, an assembly of bishops called the Convocation of Canterbury was being held at St. Paul's presided over by Thomas Bouchier, Archbishop of Canterbury.[41] It was to this Convocation, the next day, that Warwick, March and Fauconberg swore an oath in St.

Paul's that they intended nothing contrary to the estate of King Henry and that they intended to declare their innocence or die in the field.[42]

As the Yorkists prepared to leave London, Coppini issued a warning to the King. In an open letter that also reiterated that the Yorkists did not wish to harm the King, he wrote:

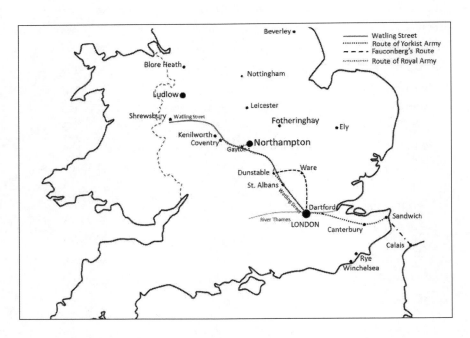

The Yorkist route from Calais to Northampton (Author)

'I beg you for the love of God, for the devotion you have always shown, which served for pious and holy things to the extent of its powers, and out of the pity and compassion you should have for your people and citizens and your duty, to prevent so much bloodshed, now so imminent. You can prevent this if you will, and if you do not you will be guilty in the sight of God in that awful day of judgement in which I also shall stand and require of your hand the English blood, if it be spilt'.[43]

As well as sending the letter personally to the King by messenger, it was posted at St. Paul's Cross, the traditional location for all important announcements.

On 4 July 1460, Fauconberg, commanding an advance guard of up to 10,000 men, left London and headed north. Warwick, securing a baggage train and a £1,000 loan from the merchants of London, left the following day at the head of the main army.[44] With them was a growing number of Yorkist supporters, including William Fiennes (Lord Saye and Sele), Henry Mountford, Sir John Mowbray (Duke of Norfolk), Edward Neville (Lord Abergavenny), John Lord Scrope of Bolton, Sir John Stafford, and John Tuchet (Lord Audley). Whilst Warwick and the Yorkist army headed north, Salisbury and Sir John Wenlock stayed behind to deal with those now trapped inside the Tower.

Battle was now inevitable.

The Battle of Northampton

Now English Bowes and Bills and Battleaxes walke,
Death up and downe the field in gastly sort doth stalke

Michael Drayton: The Battle of Northampton, Poly-Olbion 1613

We are told in both *Bale's Chronicle* and *A Short English Chronicle* that the Yorkists left with a considerable artillery train.[45] However, we are not told what it was. Nor do we do know exactly what artillery was brought from Calais and Sandwich, or what was collected on the march to London, if any. Warwick's capture of the fleet preparing to assault Calais at Sandwich earlier in the year would have, no doubt, resulted in a considerable haul.

As the Yorkists arrived in London, the Lancastrians were preparing to march south. We do not know how many people from the Royal Household were with the King and Queen, however, when the Royal Court left London for a council meeting at Leicester in May 1455; it numbered some two thousand people, including 500 fighting men of the King's own household.[46] As war loomed again, on 7 May 1459, the Queen ordered that 3,000 bowstaves, and sheaves of arrows for that many yeomen archers, were to be put into the care of Northamptonshire's Thomas Thorpe, who at the time was Keeper of the Privy Wardrobe.[47] So it is possible that at least this many archers were also in the army. In addition, Humphrey Stafford, the Duke of Buckingham, who was in command of the army, was reported to have had two thousand "Stafford Knots" (his livery badge) made 'to what intent men may construe as their wits will give them' in January 1454.[48] Whist not all of these badges would have been for fighting men, the number gives an indication of the size of the force he would have brought with him.

Also in the army was Thomas Percy, Lord Egremont who was the son of the Earl of Northumberland. There had been a private war between the Percies and Nevilles going back to the early 1450s. In August 1453, Egremont, with around 1,000 men, had ambushed a Neville wedding party near the Neville castle of Sheriff Hutton in Yorkshire. The bride was Maude Stanhope, the niece and heir of Lord Ralph Cromwell, who was also in the wedding party. His main seat was Ampthill in Bedfordshire. The King would later send a royal commission led by Lord William Lucy of Dallington in Northamptonshire to investigate the ambush. On 31 October or 1 November 1454, the Percies and Nevilles clashed again at Stamford Bridge, resulting in many dead and wounded. Lord Egremont was then captured and imprisoned by John Neville (Warwick's younger brother), only to be freed by the King. It was this feud that had led in part to the start of the wars, and it was Warwick skirmishing with the Percies that had started the battle of St. Alban's in 1455.

Other Northamptonshire men in the Lancastrian army of 1460, were Thomas Tresham, Thomas Thorpe, Sir Thomas Green, Lord Roos of Rockingham and Edmund Lord Grey of Ruthin with his household of around 50-60 men.[49] Grey was the grandson of the Grey that was involved in Ampthill, and the cause of the earlier riots in Northampton and Bedford. Edmund Grey had been promised the neighbouring manor of Ampthill by

Ralph, Lord Cromwell, but it had also been laid claim to by Lancastrian commander Henry Holland, Duke of Exeter, great grandson of John of Gaunt and son-in-law of Richard of York. Exeter had also supported Egremont against the Nevilles and at one time claimed he was next in line to the throne. Tensions between the two had been steadily rising for some time. It is likely that Exeter was also at Northampton at the King's side.[50] Ruthin's cousin, Sir John Grey of Groby, who at the time was married to Elizabeth Woodville, and who was later killed during the second Battle of St. Alban's was also on the Lancastrian side.[51] Ruthin had also managed to defraud his uncle, and Sir John Grey's father, Lord Ferrers of Groby, out of £180 (a considerable sum at that time).[52] William Catesby snr. of Ashby St. Ledger in Northamptonshire, was also fighting on the Lancastrian side, and his son, another William, would go on to achieve fame as the leading supporter of that other son of Northamptonshire, Richard III. Their descendants would achieve greater infamy as being behind the Gunpowder Plot.

The Earl of Wiltshire was almost certainly at Coventry, fresh from his sacking of Newbury. Whether he reached Northampton is unclear, as it is around this time that he fled and took a ship to Europe. Other nobles in the Royal Army included Sir John Talbot, Earl of Shrewsbury and his brother Christopher. Another was John Beaumont, the first Viscount created in England and a personal advisor to the Queen. Both Wavrin, and *Hall's Chronicle* suggest that Somerset and probably Sir Anthony Trollop were also present at the battle, although they may have not played an active part.[53] After his defeat at Pont de Neullay, there is no official record of Somerset's whereabouts until he is ordered to surrender Guînes on 7 August.

Although we do not know when the Queen and her advisors started making plans for a possible Yorkist return, we do know that Jasper Tudor was instructed by the Queen to muster men-at-arms and archers for a possible return of Richard of York through Wales as early as February 1460.[54] Commissions of Array must have been issued to all the Lancastrian supporters as soon as news of the Yorkist landings had been received at Coventry, if not before. Typically they would have been given a rendezvous point in advance and some would have mustered at Coventry before the army had left. All those who answered the summons are not recorded, except for the towns of Shrewsbury which sent fifty-one men; Coventry which sent forty men; and Beverly in Yorkshire, which sent twenty more. It is also recorded that the night before the men of Beverly left to join the King, they were thrown a party by their Mayor, and as they left the town on horseback (although they would fight on foot) they were played out by musicians.[55] Northampton's Sherriff, Thomas Wake of Blisworth, and the local troops raised by Henry's Commission of Array were either defending the town or fighting at the battle. According to the poem 'Rose *of Rouen'*, the town banner they fought under at Towton the following year was the 'Wild Rat', so we might assume they used it in 1460. Sadly no record of what it looked like survives.[56]

During the crisis of May 1455, Coventry had raised and equipped a hundred *'good-men defensibly with bows and arrows, Jakked and saletted'*. The troops were issued with new livery, *'bends'* of green and red cloth to be worn over their jacks.[57]

The recruits were also issued with a new tasselled standard which, according to the *Rose of Rouen*, bore a black ram. However, they were stood down again, as the battle of St Alban's had been decided before they could leave Coventry. Their equipment was put into storage until needed again. Like Jasper Tudor's forces, they were raised again in February 1460.[58]

It is also probable that there was a Welsh contingent at the battle. In his second passage on the battle, Wavrin discusses *'le seigneur de Greriffin'* in some detail.[59] This mysterious man has often been translated as Lord Grey of Ruthin, and consequentially the whole section of his part in the battle discounted by historians. However, as Wavrin mentions Lord Grey in a different context in his first passage on the battle, it is unlikely that he would have contradicted himself. *Greriffin* is more likely to be a translation of the Welsh name Gruffydd or Griffith. It is not inconceivable that Jasper Tudor, a Privy Councillor and close ally of Margaret of Anjou, would have sent one of his Lieutenants to aid the Queen in her hour of need. Whilst no other chronicler mentions *Greriffin* by name, Leyland's *Itinerary* does state that many Welshmen were drowned in the river after the battle. At present, it cannot be said with any certainty who Gruffydd or Griffiths was. There are, however, a number of contenders. Firstly one of the family of Sir Gwilym (William) ap Gruffydd of Penrhyn, Chamberlain of North Wales, whose wife came from Apthorp in Northamptonshire.[60] Alternatively, it may have been Gruffydd ap Nicholas who died in unknown circumstances in 1460, or one of his many sons. Records show that two of them were fighting as Lancastrian Captains in the Battle of Mortimer's Cross a little over six months later.[61] Another possibility was one of the Griffins of Braybrooke in Northamptonshire.

So with a plan in place and troops either mustered or *en-route*, the Lancastrian army left Coventry. There is some contention as to whether the Queen (and her infant son) marched with them, with as many chroniclers saying she was, as was not. Hall tells us that immediately before the battle:

"...the Quene encouraged her frendes, and promised great rewardes to her helpers' and 'When ye Kynge's host was assembled and that the Quene perceyved that her power was able to matche with the force of her adversaries, she caused her army to issue out of the town...'

The Queen was in complete control of the King and his advisors. And, with all this in mind, it is inconceivable that she would not have wanted to oversee the destruction of her enemies herself. Hall also tells us that once Margaret had addressed her troops, she retired to a safe distance, along with Somerset, possibly to the town or the nearby church to watch events unfold.

The Lancastrians arrived at Northampton several days ahead of the Yorkists, suggesting that the location was pre-planned. Bale's Chronicle notes that the royal advisors wanted the King to retire to Ely, which would be more easily defended. However, as Ely was surrounded by swamp (it was not drained until the seventeenth century), the defences were too good and the Yorkists may have refused battle. This also implies that the Lancastrians were on the defensive which, as we have seen, was not the case. In addition, the Bishop of Ely was also marching north with the Yorkists and the following year would later refortify Ely, garrisoning it with Burgundian crossbow men against the Lancastrians.[62] It may have also been deliberate misinformation supplied by the royal army, as we also read that the Yorkists followed two separate routes north. To do this, the Yorkists would have to travel up the Great North Road, which passed through the edge of the Fens. It was a dangerous road to travel at the best of times and in wet weather totally impassable, particularly around Stamford. For the Lancastrians, as well, moving to Ely via Leicester along the Roman roads was a much more direct route. A northern army, commanded by Henry Percy, Earl of Northumberland and John Lord Clifford was summonsed to join the King, but did not arrive in time.[63]

The Landscape

The Lancastrian army passed through Northampton and began fortifying a position to the south of the town close to the Cluniac Abbey of St. Mary-in-the-Meadows, better known as Delapré Abbey. The abbey had been founded by the 3rd Earl of Northampton, Simon de Senlis II, during the reign of King Stephen and held a Royal Charter from King Edward III. It was one of only two Cluniac monasteries of women built in England (the other being Arthington Priory in Yorkshire). Typically a dozen to twenty nuns resided at the abbey at any one time. At the time of the battle the Abbess was Gonora Downghton. The nuns seem to have dyed their own wool or cloth and sold it in London as it is recorded that John of the Nonnes de Norhamptone, was a draper in Dowgate during 1309-36 and Robert of the Nonnes, draper, was in Billingsgate in 1309-10.

The Guild of Weavers at Northampton made an annual procession to the Abbey church each Easter Monday where, according to the ordinances of the Guild in 1431, they would offer up "...tapers before the ymages of the Trynitie and our Lady".

Most of the landscape to the south of the abbey was farmed by the system now known as ridge and furrow, large parts of which survive today. Some has even been made into hazards for the modern golf course. However, running west to east on the northern edge of the abbey was a substantial water course with a bridge across the modern London Road. It is likely that this bridge is the one referred to in John Stone's Chronicle as "Sandyngford bregge nexte the towne" and Sandyfforde in the Short English Chronicle (see below). The County Bridge Report of 1870 says that "The bridge now forms part of the main sewer of Hardingstone Local Board and is enclosed at each end, it is now invisible and has been thus for some few years".[64] There is still a pumping station on the site (part of the model railway), however, the bridge has long since disappeared. It must have been impressive as "... the arches of old St Leonard's Bridge, the parapet of which is now standing, were culverted over, thus hiding two of the earliest and best proportioned arches in the county".[65]

The area between the Abbey and town also seems to have been built up. In the late 1940s, an aerial survey of the area revealed below the ground a huge cross shaped structure and orientated east/west, to the immediate north of the lost water course. The probable explanation for it is a substantial church, although the site requires a full archaeological excavation to confirm this. It is likely that it was the remains of this structure that authors such as Sir James Ramsay, writing in the late nineteenth century, thought were part of the Lancastrian defences in 1460.[66] The structure may have been part of the abbey but could also be part of a large leper hospital called St. Leonard's which ran between the abbey and the town. The exact date of St. Leonard's foundation is unclear, although it had received special protection from both King Henry II (1154-1189) and his son King John. Its church was unusual in that it was also used as a parish church. In the mid-fifteenth century although leprosy was declining, there were still a number of lepers at the hospital. And, in 1472, the town leased the hospital with all its lands, tenements, and rents. As part of it, the leaseholder had to pay 5d. per week to each male or female leper who might be there, and keep the church in good repair. From then on, the number of lepers fell rapidly until it fell out of use. However, at the time of the battle, leprosy was still a stigma and very few of the highly superstitious soldiers would have dared to cross its precincts.

The Fortifications

"An English Chronicle" notes that *"The kyng at Northamptone... ordeyned there a strong and a myghty feelde, in the medowys beside the Nonry [Nunnery] ... havyng the ryver at hys back"*.[67] *"The Chronicle of John Stone"* gives a detailed description of where the battle was fought. The problem is that it is difficult to equate to modern names: *"And for the feldys name of that oon parte on the northest syde it is callyd Cowemedewe. And that othir parte is I callyd Menthynfeld. And for the othir part is callyd of tyme Sandyngford bregge nexte the towne. On the est*

syde there is a water melle [that] *is called Sandford melle.*[68] Menthynfeld probably means Nuns field and Sandyngford bregge is discussed above. Sandford melle probably refers to the area now called Rushmills which is north-east of the abbey. Even in the late 19th century, the road that crossed the river and a nearby farm was called Sandyford. A Short English Chronicle, written soon after 1471, says that the battle took place *"be syde Northhampton in the Newfelde be twene Harsyngton [Hardingstone] and Sandyfforde".*[69] In his Latin chronicle, written before 1471, John Benet, the vicar of Harlington in Bedfordshire, says that King Henry's fortified camp, containing 20,000 men, was positioned between Hardingstone and Delapré Abbey.[70]

Hall, writing 100 years later, generally agrees saying *"When y kinges host was assembled, and that the Quene perceyucd that her power was able to matche with the force of her adversaries, she caused her army to issue out of the towne, and to passe the ryuer of Nene, and there in the newe felde, betwene Harsyngton and Sandifford, the Capitaynes strongely ernparked them selfes with high bankes and depe trenches".*[71]

Wavrin reported that the royal army was stationed outside Northampton, in a *"park by a little river".*[72] The River Nene at the time was substantial and probably still navigable to the sea (William Vaux's house in the town at the time was known as *le Kay* – the Quay). It would have also been wider than normal at the time of the battle due to flooding caused by the unseasonably heavy rain. In the original text Wavrin also uses the word *rivière* which means a river that flows into another river (a river that flows into the sea is called a *fleuve*). Therefore

Wavrin wrote of a little stream that flowed into a river. There is a natural spring which starts on the high ground to the south of the abbey. It runs down as a stream across the front of the abbey, although the lower part of it was culverted over some time later. One of the old fields on the bank of this stream was also called *'battle dyke'*.[73] It is therefore probable that this stream was the one that Michael Drayton wrote about in his poem about the battle called *'The Polyobion'* in 1613:-

"The king from out the towne, who drew his foote and horse, As willingly to give full field roomth to his force
Doth passe the river Nen neere where it down doth runne
From its first fountaines head, is neere to Harsington,
Advised of a place, by nature strongly wrought."

On the high ground above the abbey stands Queen Eleanor's Cross. It was from here that John Stone says the Archbishop of Canterbury watched the battle, which he says was then, as now, *'headless'*.[74] Wavrin also says that when the Bishop of Rochester approached the King's camp *"as far as a cross on a hill above the said camp, he met a gentleman of the watch"*. Another early version of the same account says *"when the bishop had come and arrived before the camp where the King and his might were lodged close to a cross that is close to a hill which was above the camp"*.[75]

The Register of Abbot John Whethamstede, of St Alban's, described the Lancastrian position at Northampton as strongly fortified camp equipped with engines of war, and in another account:-

"... a strong and a myghty feeld... armed and arayed wythe gonnys, hauyng the ryuer at hys back".[76]

According to Gregory's Chronicle it was a *"Castramatatio (military camp) armed and arrayed with gonnys"*. Wavrin recounts that when the Bishop of Rochester saw the camp he *"saw the great preparation of men at arms and artillery and the great ditches they had made around the camp, in which the water of the river flowed, which [the water] encircled the whole army"*. The use of artillery was still in its infancy and unlike later times when cannon were placed wheel to wheel, they were normally emplaced in a fortified position and protected by archers as at Crayford in 1452 and Ludford Bridge in 1459. Many of these defences were based around a river or stream. Northampton offered a number of suitable locations, due to the River Nene (Nen) and its myriad of tributaries in the valley immediately to the south of the town.

No doubt, the last battle of the Hundred Years War, Castillon, only seven years previous was still fresh in the mind of the Lancastrian commanders, as a number of them had taken part. For one Lancastrian commander at Northampton, Sir John Talbot, Earl of Shrewsbury, the memories would have been particularly bitter. His father had led the Anglo-Gascon army at Castillon and had been killed in the assault. Sir John may have even been present. What better way to destroy the 'Rebels' than catching them in a similar trap.

On Monday 7 July 1460, at about five in the afternoon, William Waynflete, Bishop of Winchester and Lord Chancellor of

England, in the presence of the Bishop of Hereford, the Bishop of Durham, Keeper of the Privy Seal and Master Thomas Marninge, the King's Secretary, as well as two esquires, surrendered the Great Silver Seal of England to the King in his tent. According to official records, this was standing in Hardingstone field. He then fled. The seal was placed in a chest in the tent, and the keys given to the King.[77]

On the same day it was reported from Bruges that the Calais Lords proposed to pass over the King's son, Edward, who was rumoured to be illegitimate, to make a son of the Duke of York king.[78]

The Yorkists march

Meanwhile, the Yorkist army was marching north. Fauconberg was heading for Ware, and Warwick with the main army was heading towards St. Alban's where they would stop for a night. According to Wavrin, en-route to St. Alban's they were joined by *"le seigneur de Scaulay"* accompanied by four hundred archers from the land of Lancaster. This was probably William Stanley who had fought with Salisbury at Blore Heath, and whose brother was with the King. There are many reasons why the army would have taken separate routes. It could have been, as Bale tells us, because they thought the Lancastrians were heading for Ely but, as we have already seen, more likely out of logistical necessity.[79] The two forces re-joined at Dunstable, where they waited two days for the infantry to catch up, naturally slower than the mounted troops, but also because of the heavy rain had slowed them.[80]

Wavrin writes that whilst they waited, a council, which included the archbishop of Canterbury and several other prelates and barons, was called to decide on what they had to do. It was concluded that the most honourable thing they could do was to send some notable person to the army of King Henry to find out from the lords around him why and to what purpose they put the king into the field. To this end John Lowe, Bishop of Rochester, was sent ahead of the army to salute the King and tell him that his cousins, the Earls of March and Warwick, had come to deliver him from the hands of his enemies, and also to warn Buckingham that he should leave the field or else they would fight him. The bishop rode until he reached King Henry. Wavrin continues:

"When the bishop had approached the camp as far as a cross on a hill above the said camp, he met a gentleman of the watch, who asked him the reason for his coming there and the bishop without fear answered him that he came to speak with the king... when the bishop found himself near the presence of the king and saw the great preparation of men at arms and artillery and the great ditches they had made around the camp, in which the water of the river flowed, which [the water] encircled the whole army."

The Bishop was led to the King's tent where Buckingham and the other lords gathered to hear what he had to say. The Bishop then asked to be allowed to speak to the King in person. However, Buckingham replied that the King was not quite in a condition to speak with him and that his message would be passed onto the King (which also suggests that the King was still ill and adds weight to the likelihood that it was the Queen who was in charge at the battle). According to Wavrin, the assembled Lancastrian lords agreed that it was very clear to them that *"the earls of March, Warwick and Fauconberg were only wishing for their own deaths, so they decided together to answer the bishop, saying that he should return to the lords who had sent him and tell them that they were no traitors at all nor disloyal to the King, but on the contrary they were there to protect him against all those who would do him harm"*.[81] *An English Chronicle* has a slightly different version of events, having Buckingham say, *"You don't come as Bishops but men of arms and if Warwick comes he shall die"*.[82]

The bishop returned to Warwick with Buckingham's answer, pleased that he had survived. When the Earl of Warwick heard the message he said to Edward, Earl of March that it was time to advance. All the captains were summoned, and they were ordered to be ready the next morning, as they and their men were to march on Northampton and face the King's army.

Hall places the next Yorkist camp between Towcester and Northampton.[83] Wavrin then says that the earls marched in such a way that they came close to the camp of the King which was in a valley below the town of Northampton, and the army of the Earl of March camped so high that they could plainly see what was going on in the army of the king.[84] If this was the case, then his camp could only have been around Hardingstone.

Negotiations continue

The next morning, when the Earl of Warwick came to the hill and saw the King's camp, he ordered two captains, John Stafford and Lord Scrope to lead the vanguard of their army until all his army was gathered. He then held another council. Both *An English Chronicle* and Wavrin say it was decided that Warwick's herald would take a message to King and his councillors to find out whether they wished to leave the field or fight. When the herald met Buckingham he responded by saying that he would not leave the field without fighting and that he would have no other answer. *An English Chronicle* also says that Warwick asked for hostages and that he would come himself unarmed.[85]

Wavrin does not mention any further negotiations, however, An English Chronicle says they continued longer with the herald returning to the King's camp saying *'that at ii howres after none, he wolde speke with hym, or elles dye in the feeld'.*[86] It continues that the Archbishop sent another bishop but instead of relaying the message, he urged the King to fight. This was probably John Stanbury, Bishop of Hereford, who was captured after the battle and held prisoner in Warwick Castle. It was the last time in the wars that negotiations preceded a battle.

Wavrin describes how, after the heralds had departed:

"...The Duke of Buckingham called together all the lords who were around the King and said to them: 'Good lords, today it is necessary for us to fight, because our enemies are marching forward', and they all replied 'we will stand our ground, because there are enough of us."

Shortly before the battle began, in accordance with tradition, King Henry knighted a number of his supporters. One was the five year old Henry Stafford, grandson of the Duke of

Buckingham. Another was Thomas Stanley, possibly leading the Cheshire archers. Henry Stafford, as Duke of Buckingham would become King Richard III's confidant and later lose his life leading a rebellion. Thomas Stanley supported the future Henry VII against Richard III at Bosworth and probably cost the King the battle and his life. The others were Thomas Dymmoke, William Tyrell, another William Tyrell, this one *"of the Beche"* (Bey), William Norrys, John of Asheton, Henry Lewys (Loys) and Thomas Thorpe. It is likely that Stanley and Thorpe were made Knights Banneret, which meant they could fight under their own banner, rather than another noble's.[87]

The Town is attacked

Three sources, Wavrin, a *"Newsletter from Bruges"*, and Hall, all write of a Lancastrian force outside the fortifications. Hall says it was Beaumont, who with a small force attacked Warwick's division as they approached, but were easily swept aside.[88] The Bruges newsletter says that there was a torrential downpour, which *"forced the Lancastrians to come out of that place and encounter Warwick"*.[89] Wavrin, in his second account of the battle, on the other hand says that it was *'le seigneur de Greriffin'*, who along with thirteen to fourteen hundred men, was outside the fortifications. He goes on to say that the Yorkists skirmished with *Greriffin* outside the town for an hour and a half. It is not clear whether the report means the whole Yorkist army or just part, but it is more likely that it was the Yorkist vanguard led by Scrope and Stafford when they first arrived. These Yorkists then assaulted the town itself which took another half hour from when *Greriffin's* men retreated. They entered Northampton by force, pillaging the town as they passed through it, no doubt in revenge for Ludlow and Newbury, before turning back to attack the fortification.[90]

It is likely that the town was partly set on fire. The possibility of at least part of the town was burned around this time is supported by archaeological evidence, although the later 1516 fire may have obscured some of it. Evidence suggests a dramatic change of occupation in the area of St. Peters Street around the time of the battle, as houses that were built in the area around the beginning of the fifteenth century seem to have replaced by tanneries soon after.[91] In addition, two years after the battle, Edward IV granted a remission from the rent the town paid to the King for twenty years, which was further extended in 1478. Richard III also granted a further remission in 1484 because the town had *"recently fallen into ruin"*.

At this point in the battle, we get a disparity between sources. Wavrin tells us that Warwick then told his commanders that all who bore the *"ravestoc noue"* (the black ragged staff - the badge of Grey of Ruthin) were to be saved for they were the men who were to give them entry into the camp.[92] *An English Chronicle*, on the other-hand says that at two o'clock, Warwick ordered that no man should lay a hand upon the King or on the common people, only the lords, knights and squires.[93] The latter, which comes from a pro-Yorkist source, sounds more like political spin in keeping with proclamations that they only wanted to talk with the King. With the talking over, Coppini raised the standard of the Roman Catholic Church in support of Warwick. Addressing the assembled army, he gave plenary remission of sins for all those who were to fight on the side of Warwick.

The Battle of Northampton by Matthew Ryan

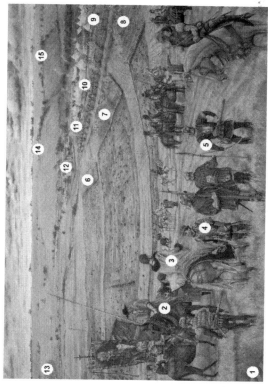

1 – The Base of Queen Eleanor's Cross from where the Papal Legate and others viewed the battle.

2 - Francesco Coppini, Bishop of Terni and Papal Legate.

3 - Thomas Bourchier, Archbishop of Canterbury.

4 - Herald wearing the arms of Warwick.

5 - Some of Warwick's guard forming protection to the clergy as the battle unfolds.

6 – William Neville, Lord Fauconberg's division

7 – Richard Neville, Earl of Warwick's division

8 – Edward Plantagenet, Earl of March's division

9 - Lord Grey of Ruthin, who defected and allowed Edward's Yorkists troops into the Lancastrian camp.

10 - Duke of Buckingham and Viscount Beaumont

11 - Earl of Shrewsbury and Lord Egremont.

12 - Delapre Abbey. (In 1460 called St Mary de la Pre)

13 - Walled Town of Northampton. Right of centre near horizon is the village of Abington and to the right of that is the Village of Weston Favell.

Annotated version of Matthew Ryan's Battle of Northampton

88

He likewise pronounced the most terrifying of all excommunications – an anathema on their enemies, exhibiting before the camp an Apostolic letter in which was believed to contain the formula for the excommunication. An ordinary excommunication entailed only cutting off a person or group from taking part in Mass and attendance at worship; however an anathema meant a complete separation of the subjects from the Church, including the prevention of a Christian burial.[94] The effect on the morale of both sides would have been seismic with Warwick's force feeling they were marching with God at their shoulder and the Royal Army suddenly seeing the mouth of Hell opening up before them, deterring anyone from fighting in case they died and spent eternity in hell.

The Two Armies

We do not know how many men faced each other that morning, although all the chroniclers agree that there were far more in Warwick's army. An English Chronicle says there were 60,000 Yorkists and 20,000 Lancastrians; Wavrin gives the numbers as 80,000 and 50,000; Bale, 160,000 and 20,000: John Whethamstede only gives the number of Yorkists, which he says was 60,000, Hall likewise puts the number as 25,000. Conversely, Benet's Chronicle only tells of 20,000 Lancastrians. Looking at Bale's numbers, whilst the 20,000 Lancastrians is consistent with everyone else, the Yorkists are wildly different. However, it is possible that over time the Yorkist number was transcribed with an extra '1', in which case, ignoring it brings Bale back in line with everyone else. Having said this, it is generally accepted that medieval chroniclers were prone to gross exaggeration when it comes to sizes of armies, so we need to look elsewhere to obtain an estimate of how many men took part. To get an idea of how many men the Lancastrian camp could accommodate, we can compare its approximate size to the size of a Roman legionary marching fort. If we take the camp dimensions as 550x260 yards, and if the area is elliptical, it gives an area of approximately 9.2 hectares, and if it is rectangular it has an area of 12 hectares. From work done by Steve Kaye in 2013, we can use the figure of 690 legionaries per hectare. This then gives us a figure of between 6,300 and 8,200 men in the camp.[95]

We can also compare the number and size of retinues. In 1458, Salisbury had 1,390 men under direct command; Warwick also employed a garrison of 1,000 at Calais around the same time. In 1475, Lord Hastings could muster 904 men and John, Duke of Norfolk's household accounts of 1483 shows that he had around 1,000 men. From these numbers, it is then safe to assume that as a rule of thumb, a duke or earl could raise approximately 900 to 1,000 men. At Northampton there were at least eight Lancastrian lords, which gives us a minimum of around 8,000 men. On the Yorkist side, using the same rule of thumb, we have nine Yorkist lords plus the men of the south east, so there must have been at least 15,000.

Many modern accounts of the battle suggest that the defenders were divided into three battles with Egremont and Shrewsbury commanding the left, Buckingham the centre and Grey of Ruthin on the right. With the number of high ranking nobles such as Beaumont, Egremont or Shrewsbury, it is unlikely that Grey of Ruthin as a minor, albeit locally powerful, lord who would have brought no more than 100 men. As a consequence he probably commanded not much more than a small section of the defences on the right-hand side. It is also possible that the Lancastrians inside the camp were not organised in divisions at all, instead they were in an all-round defence only divided by retinue.

With the forces arrayed, the stage was now set for the attack on the fortifications themselves. It was to be the only time such an assault was to happen during all 37 years of the Wars of the Roses.

Image of an armoured handgunner, wearing what appears to be a brigandine, from a contemporary manuscript. (Matthew Ryan)

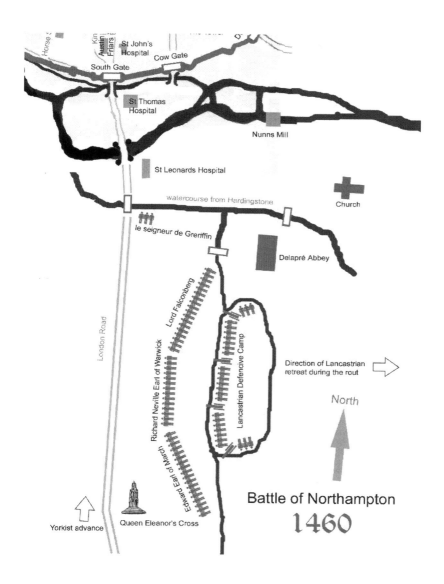

Plan of the Battle of Northampton (Matthew Ryan)

The Assault on the Fortifications

Whethamstede says that the Yorkist army divided into three battles, the first commanded by the eighteen year old Edward, Earl of March, fighting in his first battle, under the banner of his father. The second was commanded by Warwick and the third Fauconberg.[96] They attacked simultaneously along different sections of the defences, their superior numbers making an enveloping assault.[97] According to Wavrin's first account, after the Earl of Warwick gave the men their instructions, the vanguard which was led by Fauconberg, marched down the hill to the bottom of the valley.[98]

Right from the outset, things started to go horribly wrong for the Lancastrians. According to *An English Chronicle*:

"The ordenaunce of the kynges gonnes availed nat, for that day was so grete rayne, that the gonnes lay depe in the water, and so were queynt and might not be shott."

As we have seen, the Newsletter from Bruges also tells us that there was a torrential downpour, which, *"forced them to come out of that place and encounter Warwick"*. But, we also hear from Gregory's Chronicle that Sir William Lucy, who lived just over three miles away (in Dallington, now a suburb of Northampton), heard the sound of guns and came to the aid of the Lancastrians. Whether it was Yorkist or Lancastrian gunfire that was heard will probably not be known until further archaeological evidence is found, which can only realistically come from a full archaeological survey of the battlefield. However, in recent years there have been several reports of cannonballs being found on the eastern side of the battlefield which are now lost. In 2015, a 60mm lead ball, which was originally found in this area a few years previously, was identified by the author and the Northampton Battlefields Society. The ball had been severely damaged and contained particles of Northampton stone. It was analysed by Wars of the Roses artillery expert Dr. Glenn Foard of Huddersfield University, who concluded it was likely to be a cannon ball of the right period and was most probably from the battle.[99] As such it is the oldest cannonball to be found on an English battlefield to date. The find in this location also suggests that it was a Yorkist ball fired from the other side of the battlefield.

The round shot found on the eastern side of the battlefield (Author's collection)

It is inconceivable that the Lancastrians did not throw everything they had at the Yorkists when they began to advance on the camp. Even if the guns did not fire, they still had at least three thousand archers. Whilst full-plate armour would be impervious to most arrows, this would have only been worn by a small number of men. The majority, the ordinary soldier, would have worn little more than padded jacks. The effect would have been devastating.

Treachery

Those who made it to the defences had to try and scramble across the water-filled stream and the bank of earth behind. The defenders would have been stabbing and hacking down into the mass of men with swords, bills and axes, desperately trying to keep them out. At this point, Buckingham must have thought the battle was won. In living memory no army had successfully assaulted a fortified position without days of artillery preparation or by starving the defenders into submission. The chroniclers tell us that the clash continued for a half an hour, then to Buckingham's and the other earls' surprise, there came a shout from Buckingham's far left. Lord Grey's men were helping Edwards's troops over the defences and were now swarming through the position. Whethamstede writes that *"… as the attacking squadrons came to the ditch before the royalist rampart and wanted to climb over it, which they could not quickly do because of the height… the lord [Grey] with his men met them and, seizing them by the hand, hauled them into the embattled field"*.[100] Wavrin's first account says that the attack would have been harder *"if it had not been for Lord Grey who did not keep faith with the duke of Buckingham, for he let the*

95

earl of March into the camp at his side and for that reason there was great slaughter". His second account, however, only says that *"in the party of the king were several men who were for Warwick in their hearts, and even the cannoneers through evil cowardice had not put stones in their machines, wherefore when they put the fire in they only shot the wads"*. If Grey's men had only loaded wads then this suggests not only that some, if not all the other Lancastrian guns had fired, but also suggests some planning by Grey.

Wavrin's first account says that the whole battle lasted three hours and along with English Chronicle, the assault on the Lancastrian defences lasted half an hour. In his second account Wavrin gives two hours for the attack on the town, but only says the attack on the fortifications did not last long.

Grey's defection is the only part of the battle that the majority of chroniclers agree on.[101] It must have created such a stir among the people of England, and further afield, that it became the focus of the chroniclers' attention (and is probably why other actions during the battle are largely forgotten). It is not known why Lord Grey chose to defect at that point. Only Wavrin states that it had been pre-arranged although there must have been some collusion for it to happen at all. As we have seen, Grey appears to have upset many of the leading Lancastrians and would have had many enemies within the camp. There are no records of him receiving any payment in money or land in the early days of Yorkist rule, however, the dispute over Ampthill was eventually settled in his favour. It would be another three years before he was given any public recognition when Edward, who by which time was King, made him Treasurer and then two years later when he was made Earl of Kent. Perhaps he had either upset more Lancastrians than Yorkists and had decided it was time to change allegiance, or he had been bribed from Warwick's private purse. At the moment we simply do not know.

Once the Yorkists were inside the defences it was all over for the Lancastrians. Wavrin goes on to tell us there was much killing inside the camp and when the lords who were in the camp saw this, they quickly broke down a section of the fortifications to get out and fled to Northumberland. Some would have tried to reach the nearby bridge, but would have been stopped by Fauconberg's men. Many more are likely to have poured out of the camp, heading north-east as the town to the north was by this time under Yorkist control. *The Annales, An English Chronicle,* the *Short English Chronicle* and Gregory all report that many were drowned as they tried to escape by crossing the river or its tributaries swollen by the unseasonable rain. Gregory specifically says it was at a mill. The records of Beverley hint at the panic that ensued when their governors authorised 3s 4d for John Welles, gentleman, one of those sent to support the King, *"for his horse taken out of the wood killed at Northampton race by Henry Rawlin soldier"*.[102] Hall and Polydore Virgil say that many more were taken prisoner, because they had left their horses.[103] The Yorkists did not have it all their own way, as John Romney, a one-time retainer of Ralph, Lord Cromwell, petitioned the crown for the loss of his horse and armour during the battle.[104]

Buckingham was either killed outside his own or the King's tent. Shrewsbury, Beaumont and Egremont were also killed close by. Wavrin's second account on the battle says that Buckingham and the nobles including *'le seigneur de Greriffin'* were captured and beheaded after the battle. He also says it was an archer named Henry Montfort who captured King Henry.[105] Edward came to him soon after and according to An English Chronicle said:

"Most Noble Prince, displease yow nat, thoughe it hane pleased God of His Grace to graunt us the victory of oure mortalle enemyes, the whyche by theyre venymous malice have vntrewly stered and moued youre hyghenesse to exile us oute of youre land, and wolde us have put to fynalle shame and confusyone. We come nat to that entent for to inquyete ne greue youre sayde hyghenesse, but for to please youre moste noble personne, desiring most tenderly the hyghe welfare and prosperyte thereof, and alle youre reame, and for to be youre trew lyegemen, whyle oure lyfes shalle endure."[106]

No doubt this was more spin written after the event and designed to reassure the public of the Yorkist intentions.

William Lucy was a late arrival on the battlefield and although most sources only mention his death, Gregory gives us far more detail. It appears that the Yorkist knight John Strafford was in love with his wife Elizabeth. As soon as he appeared, Strafford attacked and killed Lucy with an axe. The happy couple were married soon after. However, Strafford died during the Battle of Towton the following March. It seems possible that Lady Elizabeth Lucy would go on to have a relationship with Edward IV and bore him a son, Arthur, 1st Viscount Lisle between 1461 and 1463, and a daughter. She eventually married one of the sons of Thomas Wake, sheriff of Northampton.[107]

The number of casualties varies wildly between the chroniclers. At one end of the scale, Bale puts the total at fifty-eight whilst at the other Wavrin gives a figure of 12,000. Both Virgil and Hall say 10,000. Strangely, considering how much detail is recounted, *An English Chronicle* only says that 'many' were killed and not one source mentions how many Yorkists were killed or injured. Given that, however many were really killed, Bale's number is exceptionally low compared to the rest, so he is probably only referring to the number of nobles killed. It is probable that many Yorkists were killed in their initial assault, so we must count the dead in thousands rather than hundreds. The true figure then, was quite probably suppressed by the Yorkists in an attempt to show that they did not wish to harm anyone.

Relying on folk memory, Leyland, writing some time later, does not give the number of dead. However, he says some were buried near St. John's hospital with the majority being buried close to the Abbey's church (the church was pulled down during the dissolution of the monasteries under Henry VIII).[108] St John's, was founded around 1140 for the benefit of the poor and sick as well as for orphans and passing pilgrims and was one of four hospitals close to the main gates of the medieval walled town of Northampton. The buildings consisted originally of a chapel, infirmary and a master's house. Only the chapel survives today and is used as a restaurant. The site was dedicated to St. John the Baptist and St. John the Evangelist but is more popularly known simply as St. John's. In September

1820, it was reported that 400 young and middle aged bodies were found ten to twelve feet down whilst rebuilding the 'Three Cups' (later called the Three Crowns) Public House in Bridge Street, Northampton. It had been built on the site of St. John's hospital and, at the time, it was claimed they were bodies from the battle. If they are from the battle, then they could be some of the injured or Yorkists.

The Delapré grave pits have yet to be found. But we must also remember that Coppini forbade the burial of the Lancastrian dead? If true, the nuns would not have wanted rotting corpses close the Abbey, so they would have been buried close to where they fell soon after, but on unconsecrated ground, not within the confines of the abbey or another church. Eighteenth century maps of the area show tumuli all over part of the battlefield, however, none remain as Victorian antiquarians sliced the tops of most in their search for treasure. Records show that nothing was found in them. It is just possible; therefore, that some may have been the location of the grave pits. With this premise, the Lancastrians would have been buried in the unconsecrated ground, the Yorkists in the churches. Whilst the ordinary soldier was buried in grave pits, the lords were given burials befitting their station. Although most of the nobles that were killed were taken back to their homes, Buckingham was buried at Greyfriars in the centre of Northampton. The site of the Priory has long since disappeared and in the 1970s the whole area where it stood was demolished to make way for the shopping complex that now bears its name. However, there are considerable medieval remains under the ground, so Buckingham's tomb might still be waiting to be discovered.

The view from Queen Eleanor's Cross looking east across the battlefield today. Now obscured by trees, the River Nene would have been visible from here in 1460. (Author's collection)

Aftermath

Queen Margaret and her son made their escape as soon as she saw that her cause was lost. Hall and Polydore Virgil tell us how she first fled to Yorkshire then Durham. *An English Chronicle*, on the other hand, says she fled to Harlech and then Denbigh Castle in Wales via Lancashire. In one account, whilst on her way north, she met up with the men of Lord Stanley who robbed her of all that she possessed (other accounts say that it was John Cleger, one of her servants). While the men were distracted by their booty, she managed to slip away with the help of a 14-year old squire, John Coombe of Amesbury, Margaret, her son and Coombe all riding John's horse. In the forest, they met with a brigand who seemed determined to take advantage of her position. Thrusting her son forward, she said "Save the son of your King". The man hesitated; his rough nature touched by the gesture and the plea of a beautiful woman, and then guided her towards Harlech Castle.[109]

There is also an official report that the royal treasure was indeed stolen after the battle at Gayton, which is a few miles south-west of Northampton and not too far from Watling Street, the most likely route for anyone fleeing to Wales.[110] This in turn gives extra weight to the probability that Queen Margaret was present at the battle. And, on 15 July 1460, Thomas Mascy of Podynton, William Stanley and three other men were given commissions to arrest Thomas Gless, John Glegg, and two others, who were charged with stealing 20,000 marks worth of money and jewels from the King at Gayton.

They were held at Chester Castle, but once Edward had taken the throne, were all pardoned.[111]

Coppini continued to support the Yorkist cause. However, after the death of Richard of York, he wrote a letter to one of Margaret's household, strenuously denying his actions. On his return to Rome in 1462, Pope Pius II denounced him for grievously exceeding his instructions. Because of his behaviour in 1460, Coppini was deprived of his Bishopric and sent to a papal prison.[112]

Thomas Thorpe was captured fleeing from Northampton disguised as a monk, complete with tonsure. He was brought before Warwick and thrown first into Newgate and then Marshalsea prison. When he was caught escaping soon after, he was sent to the Tower. In February the following year, he was caught trying to join Margaret of Anjou. This time he was executed by a band of Londoners in Harringay Park.[113]

Thomas Tresham managed to escape the carnage and joined up with Margaret of Anjou in January 1461, taking part in the Second Battle of St. Alban's on 17 February 1461, where he was knighted. He fought again for the Lancastrians at the Battle of Towton the following month where he was captured. Despite having a £100 bounty on his head, he only had his lands confiscated. In 1464, Tresham managed to secure a pardon, but failed to regain his lands and possessions. He again represented Northamptonshire in Parliament in 1467. However, he soon joined John de Vere, 13th Earl of Oxford, in his plot to overthrow Edward, but was caught and imprisoned in the Tower of London from 1468 until Henry VI briefly regained the throne in 1470. He was rewarded for his services and loyalty with various grants, including that of Huntingdon Castle. After the Battle of Barnet which was fought on 14 April 1471, he fled to meet Margaret of Anjou again, but was captured after the battle of Tewkesbury and executed on 6 May 1471.

Another who managed to escape was Lord Roos. He was attainted in Parliament on 4 November 1461 and went on to lead a section of the Lancastrian army which attacked John Neville's army at the Battle of Hedgeley Moor on 25 April 1464. He then took part in the Battle of Hexham on 15 May 1464. The Lancastrian army was crushed by Neville, and Roos was subsequently found hiding with Lord Hungerford in a wood. He was beheaded the next day at Newcastle for treason.

King Henry VI was at last back under the control of Warwick and the Yorkists. Almost all of those who opposed the Yorkists in the King's household were now dead, either cut down in battle or executed. With the battle over, Henry was first taken with due reverence to Delapré Abbey, where a Mass was heard, then in a stately procession led into the town, where he was kept for three days. The King was then taken to London arriving in the city on 16 July, and conveyed ceremoniously to the Bishop of London's palace. Edward rode alongside the King and a bare headed Warwick bearing the sword of state leading the way.

Within days of the battle, the Yorkists produced another poem. It described Lancastrians as the hunters being hunted by the Yorkists using their heraldic symbols such as the bere (bear) for Warwick and the buk (buck) for Buckingham.

And ensaumple here-of I take witnesse
Of certeyn persones þat late exiled were,
Whos sorow is turned into ioyfulnesse,
The rose, the fetyrlok, the egle, & the bere.
Gret games in Inglond sum tyme ther were,
In hauking, huntyng, & fisshing in euery place
Amonge lordes with shelde & spere;
Prosperite in reme than reignyng wase.

Where-of god of his speciall grace,
Heryng þe peple crying for mercye,
Considering þe falsehode in euery place,
Gaue infleweinz of myrþe into bodyes on hye.
The which in a berward lighted preuelye,
Edward, yong of age, disposed in solace,
In hauking & huntyng to begynne meryly,
To Northampton with þe bere he toke his trace.

The bere for all þe dogges wold not seese,
But hyed hym sone afftre swyfftly in hast.
The dogges barked at hem ful fast,
The buk set vp his hornes on hye;
The berward, thei cryed, thei wold downe cast,
The bere also, if that he come nye.
The bereward asked no questioun why,

But on the dogges he set full rounde;
The bere made the dogges to cry,
And with his pawme cast theyme to grounde.
The game was done in a litel stounde,
The buk was slayne, & borne away;
A-gayne the bere than was none hounde,
But he might sporte and take his play.[114]

Whilst the battle was being fought in Northampton, the siege of the Tower of London continued. Lord Cobham and the sheriffs of London attacked from the city and Sir John Wenlock and John Harowe, a London mercer, from St. Catherine's side. The Lancastrians shot wild fire, a form of incendiary not unlike modern napalm, and small cannons into the city, burning houses, killing women and children. The Londoners replied by firing a great bombard at the walls and Tower from the other side of the Thames, causing the walls to crack. Whilst negotiating surrender on 19 July, fearing for their lives, the Lancastrians made a run for it, seeking sanctuary at Westminster Cathedral. Scales was spotted and pursued along the Thames. He was eventually seized and killed in Southwark, his body dumped in the doorway of St. Mary Overie church (now Southwark Cathedral). Others were captured in Holborn and a number killed. At least seven more minor Lancastrian officials were captured and tried at the Guildhall during the last week of July by the Lord Mayor and Yorkist lords. They were beheaded at Tyburn (a traditional execution site) soon after. A Milanese observer remarked "It is not thought that he [Warwick] will stay his hand, but will put to death all those who acted against him".[115]

Once back in London, the Yorkists wasted no time in replacing those in key government posts with their own men. Bishop Neville was made Chancellor on 25 July; Viscount Bouchier, the Treasurer; Robert Stillington, Bishop of Bath and Welles, Keeper of the Privy Seal. Warwick's younger brother, John Neville, became Chamberlain, controlling all access to the King. Both Warwick and Salisbury took their reward from the

106

lands of those killed in the battle, Warwick taking control of all the Duchy of Lancaster and Buckingham lands in Northamptonshire.

Shortly after the battle, William Carnsyowe, who was known as a 'great errant Captain of Cornwall', declared that Henry Gyllyot from Helston in Cornwall was a traitor. He announced that he would hang Gyllyot at his own door and that he deserved to lose life and property because he was a traitor who had fought with the Yorkists against King Henry at the battle of Northampton. With a band of armed men, they attacked his house forcing the man to flee in only a shirt and hide in a chapel two miles away, for three days.[116]

At the same time as the battle was being fought at Northampton, the Scottish, under their King James II, took advantage of the turmoil and laid siege to Roxburgh Castle, one of the last Scottish castles still held by the English after the Wars of Independence. James took with him a large number of cannons imported from Flanders. However, on 3 August, he was attempting to fire one of these cannons, known as "the Lion", when it exploded and killed him. Robert Lindsay of Pitscottie stated in his history of James's reign that "*as the King stood near a piece of artillery, his thigh bone was dug in two with a piece of misframed gun that brake in shooting, by which he was stricken to the ground and died hastily.*" The Scots carried on with the siege, led by George Douglas, 4th Earl of Angus, and the castle fell a few days later.

York finally returned from Ireland and landed near Chester on or about 9 September. He was met at Shrewsbury by

Warwick and, after a meeting, Warwick returned to London, York to Ludlow.

Parliament met for the first time since the battle on 7 October. Their first act was to reverse the attainder pronounced at Coventry. York arrived in London four days later with 300 men wearing his blue and white livery with fetterlock badge, to the sound of trumpets with a naked sword carried before them. He also bore the whole arms of England, not his normal quartered arms on his banners. He was met by his wife Cecily, carried on a blue velvet chair.[117] Both An English Chronicle and Gregory recount that York went to the King's royal apartments forcibly taking them over and was violent towards Henry. Whethamstede says that York only broke the seals to the royal apartments and that Henry was staying in the Queen's apartments at the time.

York then went to Parliament, marching straight to the King's empty throne and laying his hand on it. Even to those not taking the hint on his entry to the City, it was now clear that Richard of York was laying claim to the throne of England. Silence befell the Parliament. The silence was only broken when the Archbishop of Canterbury asked York if he wanted to see the King. The Duke replied *"I know of no one in the realm who would not more fitly come to me than I do him"*[118] As we have seen, this may have been the plan all along, but the nobility were not happy. This was not the mandate that they had agreed to fight for. They were happy for York to run the country, not for him to usurp the throne from a crowned King. The chroniclers recount how both Warwick and York's sons, Edward and Edmund, remonstrated with him. This may, however, have been only after they had seen the nobility's response. And Edward would be happy to take the throne for himself the following year.

On 25 October, a compromise was suggested. It would be known as the Act of Accord. Henry would continue as King until his death or abdication, but his son Prince Edward would be disinherited in favour of York and his sons.

The Yorkists may have been in control of London and the south, however, the lands north of the river Trent, much of Wales and the South-West were hostile to the new Yorkist regime. The Queen was enraged that her son had been disinherited and she wanted revenge. Many important families such as the Percies, Beauforts (including the Duke of Somerset), the Earls of Wiltshire and Devon, as well as the Tudors, still supported her. Richard of York, his son Edmund and Salisbury were all killed at the Battle of Wakefield on 31 December 1460.

York's son Edward, Earl of March, then took on his father's claim to the throne, aided by Warwick and Fauconberg. What was started at Northampton, finally came to an end on Palm Sunday 1461, when the bloodiest battle in English history took place in fields outside the small Yorkshire village of Towton.

Edward, Earl of March, son of Richard, Duke of York, was crowned King Edward IV on 28 June 1461 and would remain on the throne for more than twenty years, dying in his bed in 1483. His largely peaceful reign was only interrupted by two short interludes. But those short interludes are stories for another time.

The view from Queen Eleanor's Cross looking north across the battlefield towards Delapré Abbey today. Much of the original medieval field system now known as *'ridge and furrow'* still survives on many parts of the battlefield. (Author's collection)

Northamptonshire and the Wars of the Roses after 1460

Some Lancastrian resistance continued in Northamptonshire after the battle. On 23 July 1461, John Wenlock (who had laid siege to London, a few months earlier) submitted a claim for £252.00 for himself and his men for the 'expedition to Thorpe Waterville' (three miles from Thrapston) between 17 March and 15 May 1461. On 31 March 1461, only two days after the battle of Towton, William Lee, a joiner, was instructed to find carriages and labourers called 'carters', horses and oxen for three cannon or great bombards to lay siege to the castle at Thorpe Waterville. Although it is not recorded who was inside the castle, the manor of Thorpe Waterville was held by Henry Holland, the Duke of Exeter, at the time. Wenlock seems to have found taking the castle hard because the next day Edward ordered John Wenlock to summon the gentry of Northampton, Bedford, Buckingham, Cambridge and Huntingdon to assist him in taking the castle. There are no further details of the siege, but considering the need for the cannons and summonsing of the gentry, it must have been substantial. In addition, when John Leland passed through the village during the late 1530s, he noted that the outer wall of the castle was in ruins. It is probable that they were destroyed during the fighting. The great hall of the castle still survives today and for many years was used as a barn.[119]

A force from the town under the Wild Rat banner fought for Edward in England's bloodiest battle at Towton on Palm Sunday 1461. Edward, Earl of March was crowned King Edward IV on 28

June 1461. Early the following year Edward formally pardoned the town:-

"Know ye that by our especial grace and out of our certain knowledge and mere motion We pardon remit and release to our faithful men of the town of Northampton and to the burgesses of Northampton all manner of transgressions offences misprisons contempts and violences by the same men committed before the 4th day of November last."[120]

Edward IV, seems to have had considerable affinity with the county. Northampton was the only town shown on Edward IV's ancestry roll which was written soon after his coronation. Not only that, but the badge is identical to the one used today by the county, two white roses on a red background above a red rose on a white background. In fact the whole modern county badge is Yorkist, as it also contains Richard of York's symbols, the falcon and fetterlock in it. Flanking the badge are two other key Yorkist symbols, the white hart of Richard II and black bull of Clare.

The Coat of Arms of Northamptonshire County Council with the 'falcon and fetterlock' from Richard, Duke of York's badge and the Yorkist white roses. The central shield has not changed since the fifteenth century. (Author's collection)

In 1463, having changed sides the year previous, Somerset, at the head of the King's Guard, would return to Northampton with King Edward. The people of the town made it clear that they thought Somerset was a traitor and attempted to hang him in the market square. For a while King Edward had to stand over Somerset, sword drawn. Then to placate the rioters, the King gave a tun (around 250 gallons) of Royal wine to the town. It was reported that from all around, locals began to appear with bowls of silver, which they promptly filled with the wine. With the locals preoccupied, Somerset made his escape.

Over the coming years, animosity between the Woodvilles and the Kingmaker continued to grow. It was early in 1461 that King Edward first met Elizabeth Woodville, according to legend whilst out hunting in the county. The traditional spot is marked today by an oak tree called the 'Queens Oak', just outside Potterspury, off the A5. The meeting would have far reaching consequences. The couple were married in secret in the church at Grafton Regis on 1 May 1464 and Elizabeth was crowned Queen the following year. She would go on to be Grandmother to Henry VIII and Great, Great Grandmother of Lady Jane Grey and Elizabeth I. Through her granddaughter, Queen Margaret of Scotland, she became an ancestress of the Stuart, Hanover, and Windsor dynasties. Very soon after the marriage, the Woodvilles became the most powerful family in England.

The marriage and rise in power of the Woodvilles would lead to a new phase of the Wars of the Roses and another of Northamptonshire's battles – Edgecote. In 1469, the Kingmaker rebelled against King Edward. It began with a rebel army marching down from the north and Edward sent an army under

William Herbert, Earl of Pembroke, to meet them. They first clashed somewhere near Daventry (the exact site has not been identified). The two armies then met on Danesmoor close to the village of Edgecote on 26 July 1469. To begin with, the royal army had the upper hand but, when what appeared to be Warwick's main army was seen approaching, things went disastrously wrong for them. It was in fact John Clapham from Northampton with 500 men *"gathered of all the rascals of the town of Northampton"*.[121] However, the royal army panicked and began to flee. 5,000 Welshmen including 168 Welsh Nobles were slaughtered. A ten year old Henry Tudor (future King Henry VII), then a ward of Herbert, watched the battle but managed to escape and was taken to his Uncle Jasper. The Herberts were taken and executed at Queen Eleanor's Cross, Northampton, in the presence of Warwick. Richard Woodville and his son John were also seized from their estates by Warwick and executed at the Cross.

Warwick did not stop there. Soon after River's death, his wife Jacquetta of Luxembourg who was still at Grafton Regis, was accused of witchcraft by Thomas Wake who was Sheriff of Northampton (and one of Warwick's men) and John Daunger the parish clerk of Stoke Bruerne who lived in Shutlanger in Northamptonshire. Jacquetta went before the King's Bench during January 1470 to answer the charges. She could have been burned at the stake if found guilty. However, no doubt through her daughter, the Queen's intervention; she was acquitted.

Warwick was finally forced to flee to France in May 1470 where he made an alliance with the former Lancastrian Queen

Margaret of Anjou. In an accord between Louis XI, Queen Margaret and himself, Warwick agreed to restore Henry VI in return for French support for a military invasion of England. Warwick's invasion fleet set sail from France for England at the beginning of September 1470. This time it was Edward's turn to flee. With the support of Burgundy, Edward returned in March the following year, landing at Ravenspur on the River Humber. As he marched to London, Edward stopped at Daventry and on Palm Sunday said mass at the parish church. As was normal at the time all the images and statues were covered up. As the mass began, the shuttering around an alabaster image of Edward's patron saint St. Anne burst open right in front of him. Edward took this to be a great miracle and a sign from God that he would be successful. After he said thanks for the miracle, he continued to Northampton and then London. On 14 April 1471 he met and defeated Warwick's army near Barnet. Warwick was killed trying to reach his horse. On 4 May, he then defeated Margaret and a Lancastrian army at Tewkesbury.

As well as being born in the county, it was from the centre of Northampton that Richard, Duke of Gloucester, started his bid for the throne to become Richard III after the death of King Edward IV. Two of his closest advisors, immortalised in the poem by Collingborne, "*The Catte, the Ratte and Lovell our dogge rulyth all Englande under a hogge*" also came from Northamptonshire. The Catte, being William Catesby from Ashby St. Ledger, and Lord Francis Lovell, whose family came from Titchmarsh. Many men from the county, including the Wakes and Lord Zouche, taking part in his final battle at Bosworth.

One of the first failed rebellions during Richard III's short reign was started in the then north of the county at Maxey by Lord Welles, half-brother of Margaret Beaufort, mother of the future King Henry VII. Lord Lovell would go on to lead a number of rebellions against the new king Henry VII, supported by Richard III's sister Margaret, Duchess of Burgundy, who was also born at Fotheringhay. In 1499, with the war finally over, Margaret Beaufort moved away from her husband to live alone at Collyweston, also in the north of the county. She was regularly visited by her husband, who had rooms reserved for him. She died in the Deanery of Westminster Abbey on 29 June 1509.

Order of Battle

The following is a list of those identified as taking part in the battle from a number of sources. [122] There were, undoubtedly, many more whose names will never be known. Those that were Earls, Lords or Knights etc., would have had retinues of varying sizes with them. The prelates would have also had armed retainers, although these would have been for personal protection, and probably did not take part in the battle. As well as the fighting men, both sides had large baggage trains with supporting trades such as blacksmiths, fletchers, grooms, victuallers, surgeons, hangers-on and prostitutes, etc. The King would have had the Royal Court with him too, and this could have numbered as many as 2,000 people.

The Yorkists
10,000 to 15,000 men including

Richard Neville, Earl of Warwick
Edward Plantagenet, Earl of March
William Neville, Lord Fauconberg
Edward Neville, Lord Abergavenny
Viscount Henry Bouchier
Sir Thomas Bouchier
Sir Humphrey Bouchier
William Fiennes, Lord Say
John Mowbray, Duke of Norfolk
John, Lord Scrope of Bolton
John, Lord Clinton
Sir John Stafford
John Tuchet, Lord Audley
Lord William Stanley
Sir Edmund Fitzwilliam, Constable of Conisborough Castle

Sir John Barre
John Scott, Esquire of Scotts Hall, Kent
Sir John Conyers (Warwick retainer)
Sir Peter Legh (Stanley retainer)
Sir William Parr of Kendal
Sir Thomas Vaughan
Sir Walter Wrottesley
Sir James Baskerville
Captain John Baunne
Captain Robert Horne
Henry Mountford (archer)
Henry Gyllyot of Helston, Cornwall
John Romney
Sir Lancelot Threlkeld (Warwick retainer)
Sir William Chamberlain of East Harling

The militia of Rye
The militia of Winchelsea
The militia of Canterbury
The militia of Lydd
The commons of Kent

Prelates
Thomas Bouchier, Archbishop of Canterbury
Francesco Coppini, Papal Legate
Richard Beauchamp, Bishop of Salisbury
William Grey, Bishop of Ely
George Neville, Bishop of Exeter
John Lowe, Bishop of Rochester
Sir Robert Botyll, Prior of the Knights of St. John

The Lancastrians

6,000 to 8,000 men including

King Henry IV
Margaret of Anjou
Humphrey Stafford, Duke of Buckingham
John Talbot, Earl of Shrewsbury
Sir Christoper Talbot
Sir Thomas Percy, Lord Egremont
Sir Richard Percy
Henry Beaufort, Duke of Somerset
Thomas, Lord Roos of Rockingham
Viscount John Beaumont
Edmund, Lord Grey of Ruthin
Henry Holland, Duke of Exeter
Thomas, Lord Stanley
Sir John Grey of Groby
Le Seigneur de Greriffin
Sir Thomas Tresham of Sywell, Northants
Sir William Catesby Snr. Of Ashby St. Ledger, Northants
Lord Zouche of Haryngworth
Lord Vaux of Harrowden and Le Kay
Thomas Dymmoke
William Tyrell,
William Tyrell of the Beche (Bey)
William Norrys
John of Asheton
Henry Lewys (Loys)
Thomas Thorpe, Keeper of the Privy Wardrobe
Sir Thomas Ilderton (Percy retainer)
Sir William Lucy
Sir Thomas Browne
Sir Henry Norbury (Shrewsbury retainer)
Sir John Norrys

Henry Lewes of Glamorgan
Master Thomas Marninge, King's secretary
Yeoman John Chaunteler
Sir Thomas Curwen (Percy retainer)
Sir Robert Plumpton (Percy retainer)
Sir Ralph Pudsey of Boulton
Sir Ralph Shirley of Shirley, Sussex
Sir Phillip Wentworth of Nettlestead, Suffolk
Gawen Lampleugh, Taylor of York
John Clegger or Glegg (Stanley retainer)
Sir Edmund Hampden
Sir John Chalers
Edward Longford
John Pury
Everard Digby
Sir Thomas Curwen of Workington
Sir John Huddleston of Millum (Henry VI esquire of the body)
Sir William Holland "The Bastard of Exeter" (possible)
Sir John Barre of Rotherwas
Sir John Talbot of Furnival
Sir Richard Tunstall of Thurland (Henry VI esquire of the body)
Sir Henry Green of Drayton (Northants)
Sir Thomas Green of Green's Norton
Sir Thomas Ilderton
Sir Philip Wentworth of Nettlestead
Sir Thomas Browne
Sir Ralph Shirley
Sir Walter Scull of Holt (Treasurer of the Royal Household)

The militia of Northampton
The militia of Coventry
The militia of Beverley

The militia of Shrewsbury
Contingent from Wales

Prelates
John Stanbury, Bishop of Hereford
Lawrence Booth, Prince-Bishop of Durham, Keeper of the Privy
Seal

Notes on Sources

Jehan Wavrin, An English Chronicle and, to a certain extent, Hall, all go into events during the battle in far more detail than the other chroniclers. Wavrin compiled the events in *"Recueil des croniques et anchiennes histories de la Grant Bretaigne, a collection of the sources of English history from the earliest times to 1471"*. Wavrin's tome contains two separate accounts of the battle. The second seems to be a separate report inserted in later, and does not appear in all the early editions. Although much of the early part is inaccurate, the period from 1444 appears to be different as it not only corroborates other sources, but gives far more detail and is original as it contains information not found elsewhere. Wavrin was based in Bruges, where Coppini was not only a regular visitor, but also to where he wrote copious amounts of letters before and after the battle as he was trying to forge an alliance between the English and Burgundians. It is probable that Coppini either directly, or indirectly, was Wavrin's source of information or therefore, must be considered a credible contemporary source. Much of what he wrote includes detail that can only have been obtained by eye witnesses. Hall's Chronicle, although published a hundred years after events at Northampton, is likewise a valuable source, although it represents the official Tudor view of the battle. Like Wavrin, he includes details not found anywhere else, probably due in part to his grandfather being a one-time member of Richard of York's personal staff.

Jean de Wavrin's accounts of the battle of Northampton

There now follows a new translation and analysis of Wavrin's two accounts of the battle of Northampton by Livia Visser-Fuchs

For the period of the English Wars of the Roses that Wavrin was able to include in his book (1455-1471), his text can no longer be compared to that of Pierre de Fénin, who finished in 1422, Jean Lefèvre de Saint-Rémy, who 'ran out' in 1435, nor with Enguerrand de Monstrelet, whose text ends in 1444, but still available is Mathieu d'Escouchy (covers 1444-1461), Jacques Du Clercq (covers 1448 to 1467) and particularly the so-called Monstrelet-continuator (covers 1444-1471), of whose text a number of manuscripts survive, one of them owned by Wavrin himself. The remaining fragments of the work of Georges Chastelain provide a very erratic source for comparison.

To make the 'case' of Northampton a little clearer, comparison can be made to Blore Heath and Ludford Bridge. The encounter at Blore Heath on 23 September 1459 was a Yorkist victory of which there are no detailed accounts, very few contemporary reports, and continental knowledge of the battle was very scant indeed. In the work of the Monstrelet-continuator, the event cannot be identified, Jean Du Clercq mentions the battle without naming it and adds (correctly) that James Touchet, Lord Audley (le sieur Daldely), was one of the commanders and was killed. Escouchy has no mention of the event at all, the only Burgundian report of any substance being that of Wavrin, and he actually has two texts: one very brief, clearly indebted to the same source that Du Clercq had access to, the other much longer and divided in Wavrin's narrative from the first one by a long inserted text, the so-called 'Warwick's apology'. Inserting this important narrative into the existing text confused the scribe and Wavrin himself, and they did not notice that the battle of Blore Heath ended up being described twice – assuming that they were at all aware that these two texts referred to the same battle. Though more detailed and properly constructed, and used by modern historians for lack of better information, this longer report in Wavrin's book is not reliable and gets, for example, all the names of the protagonists' wrong – this may, in fact, be mainly the result of frequent copying.

The so-called 'rout' of Ludford Bridge, a Yorkist defeat that took place less than a month later, on 12 October 1459, received similar treatment from Burgundian chroniclers; it is not mentioned by the Monstrelet-continuator, very briefly referred to by Du Clercq and Wavrin in one section of their work and at greater length in another. In this instance Du Clercq also had access to more detailed information, which may be partly due to the fact that it was the desertion of troops from Calais, led by Andrew Trollope, which made the duke of York and the earl of Warwick give up the field and retire to Ireland and Calais respectively. Word may have spread from Calais into the Burgundian lands, for even Du Clercq has a long section describing events in the English enclave after Warwick's arrival. 'Warwick's apology' covered the same events and is very detailed and dramatic, though not so much on the battle as on the preliminaries and diplomatic exchanges. Even the otherwise – at this point – very meagre text of the Monstrelet-continuator mentions the earl of Warwick's adventurous escape from the south coast of England to Calais in a little boat.

The same is the case with the important Yorkist victory of Northampton, 10 July 1460, for which Wavrin is indebted to Warwick's 'apology', which dramatises the diplomatic activity between the parties and the personal behaviour of the protagonists. Wavrin also had access to a separate, quite well-informed account of Northampton that seems to be part of another separate narrative that included Blore Heath, Ludford Bridge and Northampton and was not used by any other continental writer. This separate narrative was probably inserted into Wavrin's text when it already included 'Warwick's Apology' and broke up the natural order of events. However untrustworthy these reports are usually considered to be, and however garbled they may have been by the time Wavrin's scribe(s) used them, it is clear that they do derive from sources close to the events and some of their details may be taken seriously.

It is likely that any text that Wavrin used — including 'Warwick's Apology' — was originally sent to the duke of Burgundy to keep him informed, though how exactly the process of further 'publication' should be visualised is not clear. Wavrin's literary activities were very probably known to the dukes.

Notes

There are many minor variations between fr. 84 (the basis of Hardy's and Dupont's editions) and fr. 20358 and fr. 15491 (fr.

84 and fr. 15491 are virtually identical), but only the interesting ones are given in the notes below. Capitals, punctuation and v & u have been mostly modernised; the names about which there seems to be no doubt have also been modernised. BnF fr. 20358 does not have the second, shorter version of the account. For the long version it seems the best, but also the most discursive text, perhaps causing later scribes to abbreviate and rationalise a little.

The first, long version from 'Warwick's Apology'.

Recueil, vol. 6, bk 3, end of ch. 23 to beginning of ch. 26, ed. Hardy, vol. 5, pp. 295-301, BnF fr. 84, ff. 139v-141v. BnF fr. 15491, ff. 77v- 79v; fr. 20358, ff. 197-198.

The lords decided that Salisbury will remain in London; Warwick and Fauconberg] with many prelates and great lords marched towards Northampton to do battle with the party of King Henry, who was there in person and they [the Lancastrians] had made a very strong camp near the town, which they had fortified further because it was difficult to hold, [and it would have been very strong] if there had not been a knight called *messire Rasse Segeray* who betrayed the party of the king.

How these princes departed from London, drawing to St. Alban's, and how they send to the king in all humility. Chapeter XXIII

At the time when it was reckoned fourteen hundred and sixty, as you have heard, the earls of *La Marche*, *Warewic* and *Fauquembergue* took leave of the earl of *Salsebery*, the mayor of London and the other lords, begging them very affectionately to carefully guard the Tower of London where there were many noblemen with Lord Scales and many noble ladies, who held it for the space of three weeks; here many fair skirmishes and feats of arms were performed before its surrender, and there were many dead and wounded. After their leave-taking the princes departed from London with all their men and went to lodge in St. Alban's, ten miles from there, and on the way they met *le seigneur de Scaulay*, accompanied by four hundred archers from the land of Lancaster whom he commanded, and they [the princes] made him [*Scaulay*] very welcome, and they all stayed together that night. The next day they went to lodge at *Devistalle*, six miles from Northampton where the army of King Henry was. They stayed there [at *Devistalle*] for two days so that they could all be together, for those on foot could not go as fast as those on horseback, especially because of the weather, which was rainy.

When the aforesaid earls saw their army gathered together they held a council to discuss how they could bring their undertaking to a good end; to this council were called the archbishop of Canterbury and several other prelates and barons who were in the party, to decide on all matters what they had to do; and when they had well debated the matter among themselves they found that the most honourable thing they could do was to send some notable person to the army of King Henry to find out from the lords around him why and to what purpose they put the king into the field; so it was ordered that this message would be taken by the bishop of Rochester, who came to the council and was charged with saluting the king and tell him that his cousins of March and Warwick had come to deliver him from the hands of his enemies, and also warn the earl of Buckingham that he should leave the field or else they would fight him.

How the bishop of Rochester came to the council of the king and the answer he received.

So the bishop of Rochester, charged with going to Northampton to the king of England and his great council, took leave of the lords and rode until he came to the place where King Henry was, together with the princes and barons who accompanied him; next, when the bishop had approached the camp as far as a cross on a hill above the said camp, he met a gentleman of the watch, who asked him the reason for his coming there and the bishop without fear answered him that he came to speak with the king and his great council and that he had been sent by the earls of March and Warwick. And then the gentleman very kindly said to him: 'My lord, you are welcome, I will take you to the king to give your message and perform your task', and when the bishop found himself near the presence of the king and saw the great preparation of men at arms and artillery and the great ditches they had made around the camp, in which the water of the river flowed, which [the water] encircled the whole army, he begged those who conducted him that as soon as he had come to the king they would warn the council of his arrival, which they did immediately, for they went to speak to the earl of Buckingham, who asked them whether they knew at all why the bishop had come there and they answered they did not, and then he sent someone to fetch him [the bishop] and so he was led to the front of the tent of the king, where soon the said earl of Buckingham and other great lords came to hear what the bishop wished to put forward. And when he saw the great lordship he did them reverence by saluting them from the earls of March and Warwick and all the lords who sent him, and asked them [the Lancastrian lords] humbly to allow him to speak to the king in person, but he was answered that the king was not quite in a condition to speak with him, but if he wished for anything he should say it to them and they would let him [the king] know. When the bishop of Rochester saw that for now he was not going to speak to the king, he told these lords the reasons why he had come and what he had been charged with saying, point by point. And when the earl of Buckingham had heard and understood what the bishop had to say he drew apart and called for *messire Rasse Segray*, le seigneur de Beaumont, *le comte de Chirosbury, filz de seigneur de Thalbot*, and several other great lords to discuss the answer to what the bishop had said. When they had well pondered what the said [Yorkist] princes had put forward, they said in complete agreement that it was very clear to them that the earls of March, Warwick and Fauconberg were only wishing for/ gaining their own death, so they decided together to answer the bishop, saying that he should return to the lords who had sent him and tell them that they [the Lancastrian lords] were no traitors at all nor disloyal to the king, but on the contrary they were there to protect him against all those who would do him harm.

The bishop, having his answer as you have heard, was very joyful that he could return, without danger to his body, to the earls of March and Warwick, to whom he told what the 'governors' of the king had done, who would not allow him to speak to the king.

When the earl of Warwick heard this message he said to the earl of March that it was time to march forward; so all the captains were summoned, and they were ordered to be ready the next morning, they and their men, to draw towards Northampton; this they did well and diligently. So the army, which numbered 80,000 men, struck camp; the army of the king numbered 40 to 50,000. And the earls marched in such a way that they came close to the camp of the king which was in a valley below the town of Northampton, and the army of the earl of March camped so high that they could plainly see what was going on in the army of the king.

Here mention is made of the great battle in which King Henry of England was taken and the duke of Buckingham killed, several other great lords with him.

When the earl of Warwick came to the hill and saw the camp of the king, when he had well considered its situation, he ordered two captains, of whom one was *Jehan Staffort* and the other the *seigneur de Scrop*, to lead/move the vanguard of their army until all people were gathered; then the princes and lords held a council, in which they decided to send to the king and his councillors again to know whether they wished to leave the field or fight. To take this message Warwick Herald was sent, after he had had his orders from the lords, went to speak to the duke of Buckingham, who, when he had heard his message, knowing that the earl his [the herald's] master did not love him, answered this herald very proudly, saying that he would not leave the field without fighting and that he would have no other answer. Therefore the herald returned hastily to the lords of his party, to whom he made his report about what he had experienced with the duke of Buckingham, and then, without any more delay, they [the Yorkist lords] had their people march forward in good order to attack their enemies.

Shortly after the said herald had left the duke of Buckingham, he called all the lords who were about the king, and said to them: 'Good lords, we have to fight today, for see there your enemies who are marching forward in force'. They all answered: 'We will guard our camp, for we are enough men', and so they were, that is around 50,000 men.

And this is why they say that who reckons without his host, usually reckons twice. I say that because it is very difficult to protect oneself against a traitor, as you can hear here, for before they started the battle the earl of Warwick had said to his war captains that they should tell their men that all those who wore the ragged staff (*le ravestoc noue*) should be spared, for they were the men who were to give them entry into the camp. When the earl of Warwick had instructed his men about what they were to do, he made his vanguard march, which was led by the earl of Fauconberg, and so they descended to the bottom of the valley; and the earls of March and Warwick led the battleline (*la bataille*), which went so far forward that they fell to fighting hand to hand, and there was a great skirmish, the attack lasted for quite three hours and would have been harder if it had not been for *messire Rasse Segray*, who did not keep faith with the duke of Buckingham, for he let the earl of March into the camp at his side [of the camp], and for that reason there was great slaughter; King Henry was taken prisoner by an archer called Henry Montfort and killed were the duke of Buckingham, the *earl of Chursbury, le seigneur de Beaumont, messire Thomas Fyderme* and several other great lords; in this defeat the dead numbered 12,000 and of prisoners there was a great number.

The second, short version.

Recueil, 6, 3, 38; ed. Hardy, vol. 5, pp. 322-24, BnF fr. 84, ff. 151v-152; BnF fr. 15491, ff. 91v-92; not in BnF fr. 20358.

About the battle of Northampton where were taken prisoner King Henry and the duke of Buckingham, the *comte de Beaumont* and other great lords, of whom some were beheaded.

When the confrontation (*assemblee*) at Ludlow had thus been decided (*departie*) in favour and to the honour of King Henry, and the duke of York had retired to Ireland and the earl of Warwick to Calais, as has been said, they again gathered men to the number of 40,000 men or thereabouts. Of these they made Edward, Earl of March, son of the said duke of York, commander, and with him were the earl of Warwick, the earl of Kent, the earl of Arundel, the marquis Montague and his brother, *messire Thomas de neufville*, and others. And on the other side King Henry had the duke of Somerset, the duke of Exeter, the duke of Buckingham, the earl of Northumberland and others who were also assembled at Northampton. The guarding of this town had been entrusted by the king to *le seigneur de Geriffin* with 1300 or 1400 men, and the king and his men were in a camp outside the town on a little river. Then the earls of March and Warwick drew towards the town of Northampton, coming from Calais where they had assembled; the town of Northampton is one of the strong towns (*fortes villes*) of England. Nonetheless it was taken by assault after the captain had skirmished with them [the Yorkists] for an hour and a half; the assault lasted about half an hour from the moment *the seigneur de Greriffin* had retreated from the gate, at which point his enemies entered by force; they pillaged the town and passed through it, approaching the army of the king, which was close and which they had fortified marvellously on the river and made a very strong camp, which they [the Yorkists] immediately attacked ferociously. The assault did not take long, for there were in the party of the king several men who were Warwicks at heart / were for Warwick in their hearts, and even the cannoneers through evil cowardice had not put stones in their machines, wherefore when they put the fire in they only threw/shot the wads (tampons). When the lords who were in the camp saw this they in a very sudden manner broke a section of [the defences?] of the camp to get out and they fled to Northumberland. There were taken the king, the duke of Buckingham, the lord of Beaumont, *le seigneur de Greriffin* and others, who were soon after beheaded, and the king put under safe guard; then, that same day, the duke of York was reinstated and re-established as regent of England.

The Articles of the Yorkists, presented the Archbishop of Canterbury and the Commons in June 1460.

From *An English Chronicle of the reigns of Richard II, Henry IV, Henry V and Henry VI*, J S Davies ed. (Camden Society 1856) pp.86-90

Worshypfulle Syres, We, the duk of York, the erles of March, Warrewyk, and Salesbury sewde and offred to have come unto the kyng oure souerayn lordes most noble presens, to have declared there afore hym, for oure dewte to God and to hys hyghenesse, and to the prosperyte and welfare of his noble estate, and to the common wele of alle his londe, as trew lyegemen, the matiers folowyng, that is to say:

For the furst, The grete oppressyone, extorsion, robry, murtder, and other vyolencys doone to Goddys churche, and to his mynystres therof, ayens Goddys and mannes law.

Item, The pouerte and mysery that to oure grete heuynesse oure sayde souerayne lorde standeth inne, nat hauyng any lyuelode of the croune of Englond wherof he may kepe hys honorable housholde, whyche causethe the spyllyng of his sayde lyegemenne by the takers of hys seyde howsholde, whyche lyuelode ys in theyre handes that haue be destroyers of his seyde estate, and of the seyde commone wele.

Item, Howe hys lawes been parcially and vnrightfully guyded, and that by thayme that sholde moste loue and tendre hys sayde lawes the sayde oppressyon and extorsyone as (sic) most fauored and supported, and generally, that alle rightwysnesse and justice ys exyled of the sayde lond, and that no manne dredethe to offende ayenst the sayde lawes.

Item, That it wolle please his sayde good grace to lyve upponne his owne lyuelode, whereopon hys noble progenitures haue in dayes heretofore lyued as honorably and as worthily as any Crystyn prynces ; and nat to suffre the destroyers of the sayde londe and of his trewe sugettes to lyue theroponne, and therefore to lacke the sustenaunces that sholde be bylongyng to hys sayde estate, and fynde hys sayde householde opponne his pore communes withoute payment, whyche nouther accordethe wyth Goddes nor mannes lawe.

Item, Howe ofte the seyde commones haue ben gretely and merueylously charged with taxes and tallages to theyre grete enporysshyng, whereof lytelle good hathe eyther growe to the kyng or to the saide londe, and of the moste substaunce therof the kyng hathe lefte to his part nat half so moche and other lordes and persones, enemyes to the sayde commune wele, haue to theyre owne vse, suffryng alle the olde possessyons that the kyng had in Fraunce and Normandy, Angew and Meyne, Gascoyne and Guyene, wonne and goten by his fadre of moste noble memory, and othir hys noble progenitors, to be shamefully loste or solde.

Item, How they cannat cece therewith, but nowe begynne a new charge of imposiccione and tallages vpponne the sayde peple whyche neuer afore was seen ; that ys to say, euery tounshyp to fynde men for the kynges garde, takyng ensample therof of oure enemyes and aduersaryes of Fraunce : whiche imposicione and tallage yef hit be continued to theyre heyres and successours, wol be the heuyest charge and worst ensample that euer grewe in Englond, and the forseyde sugettes, and the seyde heyres and successours, in suche bandoin as theyre auncetours were neuer charged with.

135

Item, Where the kyng hathe now no more lyfelode oute of his reame of Englond but onely the londe of Irelond and the toune of Caleys, and that no kyng crystened hathe suche a londe and a toune withoute hys reaume, dyuers lordes haue caused his hyghenesse to wryte lette^ vnder his priuy seale vnto his Yrisshe enemyes, whyche neuer kyng of Englond dyd heretofore, wherby they may haue comfort to entre in to the conquest of the sayde londe ; whiche letters the same Yrysshe enemyes sent vn to me the sayde duke of York, and merueled gretely that any suche letters shuld be to theym sent, spekyng therinne gret shame and vylony of the seyde reme.

Item, In like wyse, the kyng by excytacione and laboure of the same lordes wrote other letters to his enemyes and aduersaryes in other landes, that in no wyse thay shold shew eny favoure or good wylle to the toun of Caleys, whereby they had comfort ynowghe to procede to the wynnyng therof ; considered also, that hit ys ordeyned by the laboure of the sayde lordes, that nowther vetayle ner other thyng of refresshyng or defens shulde come oute of Englond to the socoure or relyef of the sayde tonne, to thentent that they wolde haue hyt lost, as yt may opynly appere.

Item, It ys denied, and oweth gretely to be douted, that after that, the same lordes wolde put the same rewle of Englond, yef they myghte haue theyre purpos and entent, in to the handes and gouernaunce of the seyde enemyes.

Item, How continuelly, syth the pytyous, shamefulle, and sorowfulle murther to alle Englond, of that noble, worthy, and Crystyn prince, Humfrey duk of Gloucestre the kynges trew vncle, at Bury, hit hathe be labored, studyed, and conspyred, to haue dystroyed and murthryd the seyde duke of York, and the yssew that it pleased God to sende me of the royalle blode; and also of vs the sayde erlys of Warrewyk and Salysbury, for none other cause but for the trew hert that God knoweth we euer haue borne, and bere, to the profyte of the kynges estate, to the commone wele of the same reame, and defens therof.

Item, How the erles of Shrouesbury and Wylshyre, and the lorde Beaumount, oure mortalle and extreme enemyes, now and of long tyme past, hauyng the guydyng aboute the most noble persone of oure sayde souuerayn lorde, whos hyghenes they haue restrained and kept from the liberte and fredom that bylongethe to his seyde astate, and the supporters and fauorers of alle the premysses, wolde nat suffre the kynges seyde good grace to resceue and accepte [us] as he wolde haue done, yet (sic) he myghte haue had his owne wylle, in hys sayde presence dredyng the charge that wolde haue be layde vpponne theym of the mysery, destruccione, and wrechednesse of the sayde reame, wherof they be causes, and nat the kyng, whiche ys hymself a[s] noble, as vertuous, as ryghtewys, and blyssed of dysposicione, as any prince erthely.

Item, The erles of Wylshyre and Shrouesbury, and the lorde Beaumount, nat satysfyed nor content with the kynges possessyouns and hys good, stered and excyted his sayde hyghenesse to holde hys parlement at Couentre, where an acte ys made by theyre prouocacioun and laboure ayenst vs the sayde duk of York, my sones Marche and Rutlande, and the erles of Warrewyk and Salysbury, and the sones of the sayde erle of Salysbury, and meny other knyghtes and esquyers, of diuerse matiers falsly and vntrewly ymagened, as they wolle answere afore Almyghty God in the day of Dome ; the whyche the sayde erles of Shrouesbury and Wylshyre and the lorde Beaumount prouoked to be maad to thentent of oure destruccione and of oure yssew, and that thay myghte haue oure lyfelode and goodes, as they haue openly robbed and dyspoyled alle oure places and oure tenementes, and meny other trew men ; and now precede to hangyng and drawyng of men by tyranny, and wolle therinne shewe the largenesse of theyre vyolence and malyce as vengeably as they can, yef no remedy be prouyded at the kynges hyghenesse, whos blessednes ys nother assentyng ne knowyng therof.

We therfore, seyng alle the sayde myscheues, heryng also that the Frensshe kyng makethe in hys lande grete assemble of hys peple whyche ys gretely to be drad for many causes, purpose yet ayene with Goddes grace [to] offre us to come ayene to the sayde presence of oure sayde souuerayn lorde, to opene and declare there vn to hym the myscheues aboue declared, and in the name of the land to sew in as reuerent and lowly wyse as we can to hys seyde good grace,   and to haue pyte and compassione uppon hys sayde trew sugettys, and nat to suffre the same myscheue} to regne upponne theym.

Requiryng yow on Goddys behalf and prayng yow in oure oune thereinne to assyste vs, doyng alwey the dewte of ligeaunce in oure personnes to oure sayde souuerayne lorde, to hys estate, prerogatyf, and preemynence, and to thasuerte of hys most noble persone, where- vnto we haue euer be and wylle be trew as any of his sugettes alyue :

Whereof we call God, our Lady Saynt Mary and alle the Sayntes of heuene vn to wyttenesse and record

Selected Contemporary accounts of the battle

An English Chronicle

An English Chronicle of the reigns of Richard II, Henry IV, Henry V and Henry VI, J S Davies (ed.) (Camden Society, 1856)

"The kyng at Northamptone lay atte Freres [Friars], and had ordeyned there a strong and a myghty feeld, in the medowys beside the Nonry, armed and arayed wythe gonnys, hauyng the ryuer at hys back.

The erles with the nombre of lx Ml, as it was sayd, came to Northamptone, and sent certayne bysshps to the kyng besechyng hym that in eschewyng of effusyone of Crysten blood he wolde admytte and suffre the erles for to come to his presence to declare thaym self as thay were. The duk of Bukynghame that stode besyde the kyng, sayde unto thaym, 'Ye come nat as bysshoppes for to trete for pease, but as men of armes;' because they broughte with thayme a notable company of men of armes. They answered and sayde, 'We come thus for suerte of oure persones, for they that bethe aboute the kyng bythe nat oure frendes.' 'Forsothe,' sayde the duk, 'the erle of Warrewyk shalle nat come to the kynges presence, and yef he come he shalle dye.' The messyngers retorned agayne, and tolde thys to the erles.

Thanne the erle of Warrewyk sent an herowde [herald] af armes to the kyng, besechyng that he myghte haue ostages of saaf goyng and commung, and he wolde come naked to his presence, but he myghte nat be herde. And the iiide tyme he sente to the kyng and sayde that at ii howres after none, he wolde speke with hym, or elles dye in the feeld.

The archebysshoppe of Caunterbury sent a bysshoppe of this lond to the kyng with an instruccione, the whyche dyd nat hys message indyfferently, but exorted and coraged the kynges part for to fygte, as thay sayde that were there. And another tyme he was sent to the kyng by the commones, and thanne he came nat ayene [again], but pryuely departed awey. The bysshop of Herforde, a Whyte Frere, the kynges confessoure, ded the same: wherfore after the batayle he was commytted to the castelle of Warrewyk, where he was long in pryson.

Thanne on the Thursday the Xth day of Juylle, the yere of oure Lorde Mlcccclx, ay ii howres after none, the sayde erles of Marche and Warrewyk lete crye thoroughe the felde, that no man should laye hand vpponne the kyng ne on the commune peple, but onely on the lordes, khyghtes and squyers: thenne the trumpettes blew vp, and bothe hostes countred and faughte togedre half an oure. The lorde Gray that was the kynges vawewarde, brake the feelde and came to the erles party, whyche caused sauacione of many a mannys lyfe: many were slayne, and many were fled, and were drouned in the ryuer.

The duk of Bukyngham, the erle of Shrouesbury, the lorde Beaumont, the lorde Egremount were slayne by the Kentysshmen besyde the kynges tent, and meny other knyghtes and squyers. The ordenaunce of tyhe kynges gonnes avayled nat, for that day was so grete rayne, that the gonnes lay depe in the water, and so were queynt and myghte nat be shott."

Bale's Chronicle

Six Town Chronicles of England, R. Flenley (ed.) (Oxford 1911)

And on the friday and Saterday suyng they brake agein and departed in two weyes that is to wite oon wey toward Seint

Albons and that other wey toward Ware because that the seid lordes wold mete wt the king and countre wt his ost and lett and stopp them their entre into the Isle of Ely, wher then the kings counceill hadde proposed as was seid to have left the king and for their strength and saufgard ther to have hiden. But in as moche as the kings counseill might not opteyn that purpose they set a feld beside Northampton and thedir cam the seid lordes and their peple departed in iiii Batailles and ther was nombred than of them C lx M and of the kings Ost xx M. And on the thursday was Bataill in which wer slain in the kings Ost the Duk of Buk, the Erle Shrovesbury the lord Beaumond the lorde Egremond and many other gentiles and of other to the nombre of I [50] persones and on the other partie not over viii persones...

A Short English Chronicle

A Short English Chronicle in *Three Fifteenth-Century Chronicles with Historical Memoranda by John Stowe*, (Camden Society, 1880)

"...Erle of Marche, and the Erle of Warwyke, the Lord Faconbryge, the Lorde Bowser, and his sonnes, with myche other pepull of Kent, Southesex, and Esex, tawarde the Kynge with grete ordenaunce; and the Erle of Salysbury, the Lorde Cobham, and Sir John Wenlock, were lefte in the cite of London with the meire. And forthe with the Lord Cobhamand the shoreffes went and laide grete ordenaunce a yenes the Toure on the towne syde, and Sir John Wenlok, an[d] Harow mercer, kept on Seint Katerynes side, and myche harme done on bothe parties. And in all placis of London was grete watche for doute oftresoun. And then they skyrmysed to gedir, and myche harmewas done dayly. And on the Thorsdye, the ixth day of

Julle, was the bataylle be syde Northhampton in the Newfelde between Harsyngton and Sandyfforde, and ther was the kynge take in his tente. And ther was slayne the Duke of Bockyngham, the Erle of Shrovysbury, the Vycounte Bemonde, the Lord Egremonde, and Sir William Lucy, and many other knyghtes and squyers, and many comyners were drowned. And then the Erle of Marche, and the Erle of Warwyke, with oþer lordis, brought the kynge to Northampton with myche rialte."

Gregory's Chronicle

Gregory's Chronicle in *Historical Collections of a Citizen of London*, J. Gairdner (ed.) (Camden Society, 1876)

"...so forthe to Northehampton. And there they mete with the kynge and foughte manly with the kyngys lordys and mayny, but there was moche favyr in that fylde unto the Erle of Warwycke. And there they toke the kynge, and made newe offycers of the londe, as the chaunceler and tresyrar and othyr, but they occupyde not fo[r]the-with, but a-bodea seson of the comyng of Duke of York owte of Irlonde. And in that fylde was slayne the Duke of Bokyngham, stondyng stylle at hys tente, the Erle of Schrovysbury, the Lord Bemond, and the LordEgremond, with many othyr men. Ande many men were drownyd by syde the fylde in the revyr at a mylle. And that goode knight Syr Wylliam Lucy that dwellyd be-syde Northehampton hyrde thegonne schotte, and come unto the fylde to have holpyn [t]e kynge,but the fylde was done or that he come; an one of the Staffordyswas ware of hys comynge, and lovyd that knyght ys wyffe andhatyd hym, and a-non causyd hys dethe."

Leland

Toulmin Smith, L. (Ed.), The Itinerary of John Leland in or about the years 1535-1543, 1907-10, I, 8.

'There was a great bataille faught in Henry the vi. tyme at Northampton on the hille withoute the Southe Gate, where is a right goodly crosse, caullid, as I remembre, the Quenes Crosse, and many Walsch men were drounid yn Avon (sic) Ryver at this conflict. Many of them that were slayn were buried at de la Pray and sum S.John's Hospitale.'

Polydore Vergil

Three books of Polydore Virgil, Sir H. Ellis (ed.)(Camden Soc., 1844)

"Then Warwick, seeing that his enemies posed no danger, crossed over to Ireland to the Duke of York and consulted, dealt, and deliberated with him about what to do. This done, he promptly returned to Calais and reported to his father and Earl Edward of March that the duke's opinion that they should cross over to England with a ready army and, omitting no opportunity for successful action, to trouble King Henry with their fighting until he himself could come to their aid with a large number of soldiers. They liked this plan, and, coming over to England, set out for London. For this city was not strengthened by any garrisons, nor did it abound in equipment for war, and so it was of necessity open to all comers. Here they armed men of the lower classes and whoever else came running to them, prepared the other things needful for war, then with their assembled army they marched on Northampton, where the king had come a little earlier. The queen, learning of these things, and aided by the resources of the Dukes of Somerset and Buckingham (since she was more concerned about things of this kind than was the king, for he acquiesced in her decisions alone), assembled an army with high spirits, summoning nobles of her faction from all over, who each made his appearance with a company of armed men, and in a short time she assembled her forces. The king, after discovering that, thanks to the efforts of the queen and the dukes, he was in possession of no mean army, decided to come to blows with his enemies, and encamped outside the town in the nearby meadows, along the river Nene. And when he had learned the enemy was at hand, he went to meet them and gave the signal for battle. The enemy did not shun a fight. The battle was joined early in the morning, and it was now noon when the king was defeated. A little less than 10,000 died in that fight, including Duke Humphrey of Buckingham, John Talbot Earl of Shrewsbury, an outstanding young man who resembled his ancestors, Thomas Lord Egremont, and very many others. And the number of those captured was very great, because many horsemen had elected to send away their horses and fight on foot, as was their habit. Above all, King Henry fell into his enemies' clutches, a man born for human misery, calamity, and woe. The rest of the nobles who escaped this catastrophe, together with the queen and Prince Edward, fled to Yorkshire, and thence to County Durham, so that there they might rebuild their army, or, if there was no hope for renewing the war at present, continue on to Scotland, there to await until a better opportunity for success was offered. The victorious earls led Henry to London as a captive. Then they convened a parliament and arranged for his deposition. The Duke of York, assured of this victory, immediately appeared out of Ireland, and, entering the parliament, sat in the king's chair."

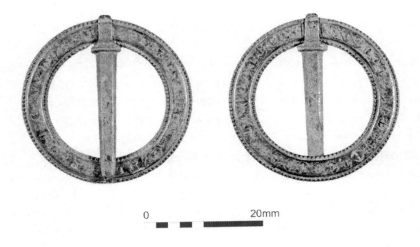

0 ▬ ▬ ▬ 20mm

The "Delapré Broach" found on the eastern side of the battlefield during archaeological investigations in 2015 and may have been lost during the rout in 1460. This type of brooch is known as an *"afermail"*, a late medieval English or French brooch worn by both sexes to close a robe at the throat in the late fourteenth, and fifteenth centuries. There is an inscription in Lombardic, or 'black', lettering saying *"en qui ne l'oublie pas, Jesus adore"* (In whom do not forget, beloved Jesus). (Source: Creative Commons via Portable Antiquities Scheme)

Northampton Battlefields Society

The Society was established in 2014 in order to promote and preserve Northampton's rich history and, in particular, it's Battlefields Heritage. Membership is open to anyone who holds an interest in history and is committed to safeguarding the heritage of Northampton. The Society has a number of aims and objectives which can be seen in full in the Society's Constitution. In short they include:

a) Advance public education through the promotion, encouragement, development and dissemination of knowledge of the history and battles of Northampton and their landscapes, as well as the associated wars and warfare.

b) Undertake and support research into the history, battles and their landscapes, the associated wars and warfare and the publication of the results of such researches.

c) Encourage the identification, protection and preservation of such sites.

The Society normally meets once a month at the Marriott Hotel, Northampton which is on the battlefield and has nationally known speakers on a variety of subjects.

For more details, the latest news, and membership details please visit our website:
https://northamptonbattlefieldssociety.wordpress.com/

or our facebook page
https://www.facebook.com/groups/Northampton1460/

Once a year, on the anniversary of the battle, members of the society, reenactors and members of the public walk from Delapré Abbey to Queen Eleanor's Cross and lay flowers for of all those who died in battle on 10 July 1460. (Phil Steele)

The Battlefield Today

The vast majority of the site of the battle is now a golf course and parkland with Delapré Abbey at its heart. It is now owned and managed by Northampton Borough Council. The largest part of the battlefield was given over to a golf course in 1976 and Delapré Golf Complex was built off Eagle Drive at the same time. A number of high banks and ditches have been created to protect the golf course and under one of these is the site of a Roman kiln. Large tracts of this land is now wooded although 'ridge and furrow' still remains within some of these areas. There are a number of tracks through these woods. Since the dissolution of the monasteries the Abbey was extensively modernised by successive generations, and little of the original nunnery remains today. In 2014, work began to restore the long neglected abbey, including a battlefield visitor centre (open summer 2016).

The area from the north of Delapré Park to the river has now largely been developed for housing and a new university complex. Part of the site of St. Leonard's Leper Hospital is now a supermarket and garage, whilst the site of the lost bridge on the north-east corner is now a Model Railway and sewer pumping station. The River Nene has itself been canalised to follow a new course to the south and to form a lake. The lake which is located in the north-eastern section of the battlefield was formed as a result of gravel extraction in the late 20th century.

On the eastern side of the battlefield is the All-work Equestrian Centre based around a nineteenth century model farm. In the mid-1970s, a hotel complex was built next to the farm. Archaeological work prior to construction revealed it was on the site of Roman buildings and a possible Neolithic cursus. To the south and east of the battlefield area is the A45 duel carriageway, part in a cutting, and part elevated with a large industrial estate to its east.

In 1995, English Heritage (now Historic England) began the Battlefield Register, listing 46 of the most significant battlefields in England. The site of the battle was therefore considered to be a heritage asset of the highest significance and was registered on 6 June 1995. It was also amended to reflect later research in April 2015. The Registered Battlefield today covers 237 hectares (586 acres), and while approximately 70 hectares (173 acres) has been disturbed or destroyed, there remains a considerable level of survival of the historic landscape. Significantly, the site is the only medieval battlefield in England where earthwork ridge and furrow, has survived over a large area.

In 2012, Northampton Borough Council commissioned LUC in association with Dr. Glen Foard and Tracey Partida to produce a Conservation Management Plan (CMP) for the whole of the battlefield. The report was published in June 2014 and can be downloaded from:
http://www.northampton.gov.uk/info/200207/building-conservation-and-trees/1952/site-of-the-battle-of-northampton-1460

Despite the CMP, this battlefield along with Edgecote battlefield remains under threat of development.

Location of the battlefield

Grid Reference: SP763594 (476351,259426)

OS Landranger map: 152

OS Explorer map: 207 & 223

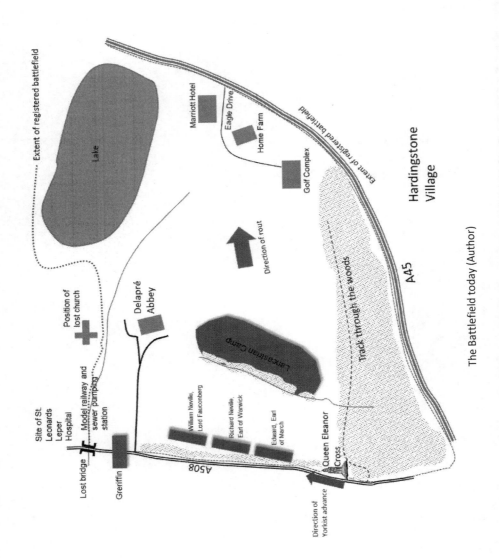

The Battlefield today (Author)

Lake

Marriott Hotel

Eagle Drive

Home Farm

Golf Complex

Hardingstone Village

A45

Extent of registered battlefield

Extent of registered battlefield

Direction of rout

Track through the woods

Position of lost church

Delapré Abbey

Lancastrian Camp

Model railway and sewer pumping station

Site of St. Leonards Leper Hospital

Lost bridge

Greyffin

William Neville, Lord Fauconberg

Richard Neville, Earl of Warwick

Edward, Earl of March

A508

Queen Eleanor Cross

Direction of Yorkist advance

Glossary

Bombard A type of large cannon usually used for sieges.

Calais Last English town in mainland Europe

Commission of Array An order sent out by the King for each town to muster its local militia. Commissioners were usually experienced soldiers, appointed by the crown

Commission of Oyer and Terminer To make diligent inquiry into all treasons, felonies and misdemeanours whatever committed, in the towns and counties specified in the commission, and to hear and determine the same according to law.

Division Medieval English armies were normally divided into three divisions, sometimes called Battles. They were known as the Vanguard (Vanward), Middleguard (Middleward) and Rearguard (Rearward). The Vanguard could mean either the first, right-hand or best division.

Fletching The feathers of an arrow.

Hanseatic League A commercial confederation of merchant guilds and their market towns along the northern coast of Europe, from the Baltic to the North Sea.

Livery Clothing and or a badge given out by a noble, lord or knight to denote membership of his retinue.

Lubeck Salt Fleet A fleet taking salt from the Baltic to Bordeaux, and then returning with wine.

Referendarius A papal representative whose duty was to receive all petitions directed to the Holy See, to report on them to the pope and to tender him advice.

Retinue Members of a noble's, lord's or knight's household. Not all would be fighting men and would include lawyers, surgeons, minstrels etc.

Serpentine Type of Cannon

Primary Sources and Abbreviations

Annales —*Annales Rerum Anglicarium in Letters and Papers Illustrative of the Wars of the English in France, Formally attributed to William of Worcester, Vol. 2,* J Stevenson (ed.) (Rolls Series, 1864)

Arrivall - *Historie of the Arrivall of Edward IV*, R Bruce (ed.) (London, 1838)

Benet - *Benet's Chronicle: John Benet's Chronicle for the years 1400 to 1462*, G.L.Harriss and M.A.Harriss (eds.), in Camden Miscellany, vol. XXIV (London, 1972)

Brut or Chronicle of England, F.W.D Brie (ed.) (Early English Text Society, 1908)

CSP - *Calendar of State Papers and Manuscripts in the Archives and Collections of Milan 1385-1618*, A.B Hinds (ed.) (London, 1912)

Eng Chron - *An English Chronicle of the reigns of Richard II, Henry IV, Henry V and Henry VI,* J S Davies (ed.) (Camden Society, 1856)

Sir J. Fortescue, *De Laudibus Legum Angliae*, F. Grigor (trans.) (London 1917)

Gregory - Gregory's Chronicle in *Historical Collections of a Citizen of London*, J. Gairdner (ed.) (Camden Society, 1876)

Hall - *The Union of the two noble and Illustrious families of Lancaster and York,* Edward Hall, (London, 1809)

Dominic Mancini, *The Usurpation of Richard III*, C.A.J Armstrong (ed. And trans.) (Oxford, 1969, reprint Gloucester, 1984)

Paston - *The Paston letters, 1422-1509 A.D.: a reprint of the edition of 1872-5*, Vol. 1, James Gairdner (ed.) (Edinburgh, 1910)

Short - *A Short English Chronicle in Three Fifteenth-Century Chronicles with Historical Memoranda by John Stowe,* (Camden Society, 1880)

Six - *Six Town Chronicles of England*, R. Flenley (ed.) (Oxford 1911)

Stone - *The Chronicle of John Stone*, W.G.Searle (ed.) (Cambridge 1902)

Stowe - *The Annales of England,* J. Stowe, (London, 1605).

Three books of Polydore Virgil, Sir H. Ellis (ed.)(Camden Soc., 1844)

Wavrin - Jehan de Wavrin, *Recuiel des Croniques et Anchiennes Istories de la Grant Bretagne, a present nomme Engleterre*, Vol. V, W. Hardy and E. Hardy (eds.) (Rolls Series, 1891). New translation by L. Visser-Fuchs

Whet — J Whethamstede, Register in Registra quorundam Abbatum Monasterii S Albani ed. H.T. Riley (Rolls Series 1872)

Endnotes

[1] Sir Charles Oman, *The Art of War in the Middle Ages* (London, 1924) vol 2, p. 408

[2] *Household books of John Duke of Norfolk* J.P. Collier (ed.) (London, 1884), pp. 480-92

[3] A. Goodman, *The Wars of the Roses* (London, 1981), p.141

[4] A. Boardman, *The Medieval Soldier in the Wars of the Roses* (Stroud, 1988), p.131. It is probably this armour that can be seen on his tomb at Dodford, Church in Northants today.

[5] Paston, pp. 486-487⬚

[6] Commynes Memoirs ed and trans Jones p. 72

[7] D. Grummitt, *The Calais Garrison: War and Military Service in England, 1436-1588* (Woodbridge, 2008)

[8] Sir J. Fortescue, *De Laudibus Legum Angliae* F. Grigor (trans.) (London 1917), pp. 56-57

[9] Exactly what type of gun this was has now been lost except that it was made of copper-alloy, but must have been large as it required eight horses to pull each one. This is the first mention of this type in the Burgundian records.

[10] R.D Smith and K. Devries The Artillery of the Dukes of Burgundy 1363-1477 (Woodbridge 2005) pp. 351-352

[11] Arrivall, p. 14

[12] CSP, p. 100

[13] Mancini, pp. 98-101

[14] Gregory, p.205

[15] Ibid, p. 213

[16] Registrum, pp. 388-92

[17] Arrivall, p.30

[18] CSP, p. 100

[19] Eng Chron, p. 81

[20] *Rotuli Parliamentorum*, Vol. V, John Strachey (ed.) (London, 1767–77) p. 348

[21] Eng Chron, pp. 81-83

[22] Wavrin p. 308

[23] N. Pevsner, B. Cherry, Bridget. *The Buildings of England: Northamptonshire. London and New Haven* (revised) (London, 1961), pp. 101–103. Barnwell Castle built around 1266, is now private property but can be seen from the road.

[24] Eng Chron, p. 84; Gregory, p. 206; Brut p. 528

[25] Gregory, p.206; Brut p. 528

[26] Paston, pp. 505-506

[27] M. Mercer, *The Medieval Gentry: Power, Leadership and Choice during the*

Wars of the Roses, (London, 2011) p.79

[28] Eng Chron, pp. 86-90

[29] Ibid, p. 91

[30] Ibid p. 93

[31] *Knyghthode and Bataile,* R. Dyboski (ed.), (Early English Text Society, 1936) p. 37

[32] Whet, p. 331

[33] CSP, pp. 21-37

[34] ibid

[35] Pius II, *Commentaries*, Vol II, M. Meserve, M. Simonetta (eds.) (Cambridge Mass, 2007), p. 269

[36] Sir H Ellis, *Original letters, illustrative of English history*: ser.III (London, 1825), pp. 82-88

[37] Stone, p. 79; Short p. 73; Eng Chron p.95; Wavrin, pp. 292-3; Calendar of Patent Rolls, 1452-61 (HMSO, 1911) p. 561.

[38] A. Goodman, Op. Cit, p.35

[39] Six, p. 149; Whet, p. 370; Annales, p. 772

[40] Annales p. 772-773

[41] Eng Chron, pp. 94-95

[42] Ibid, p. 95, Annales p. 773

[43] CSP, item 37

[44] J. Gillingham, *The Wars of the Roses*, (London, 1981) p. 111

[45] Six, pp. 150-1, Three, p. 74.

[46] A. Boardman, *The First Battle of St. Albans* (Stroud, 2006), pp. 55-56. The royal court only reached St. Albans when they were intercepted by a Yorkist army leading to the first battle of the Wars.

[47] B. Wolfe *Henry VI*, (London, Methuen, 1983) p. 317

[48] Paston, p. 265

[49] M. Mercer, *The Medieval Gentry: Power, Leadership and Choice during the Wars of the Roses*, (London, 2011) p.52

[50] http://www.towton.org.uk/wp-content/uploads/database_war_roses_combatants.pdf accessed 13/04/15

[51] ibid

[52] I. Jack, '*A Quincentenary: The Battle of Northampton, 1460*' Northamptonshire Past and Present, Vol III (1960) p 24n

[53] Hall, p. 244

[54] *Foedera,Conventiones, Litterae* ed, T Rymer, vol. II (London, 1818) pp. 444-445

[55] *HMC MSS of Shrewsbury Corporation*, p. 29; G. Poulson *Beverlac*, I (London, 1829)

[56] *Archaeologia: or miscellaneous tracts relating to antiquity*, Vol XXIX Society

of Antiquaries (London, 1842), pp. 343-347

[57] *The Coventry Leet Book,* M. Dormer-Harris (ed. and trans.), (London, 1907) p 282-3

[58] *Ibid* p 308

[59] Wavrin, p 309

[60] http://www.ffish.com/family_tree/Pedigrees/878.htm

[61] H.T. Evans, *Wales and the Wars of the Roses,* (Frome, 1998), pp 5-9

[62] Three, pp. 72, 76, 155,

[63] P.A Haigh, *The Military Campaigns of the Wars of the Roses,* (Stroud, 1995) p. 25

[64] E.F Law, *County Bridge Report, 1870* (with later additions), County Records Office. See also A V Goodfellow, The Bridges of Northampton, Northamptonshire Archaeology Vol 15, (NAS, 1980) p. 139

[65] J T' writing in the Northampton Herald newspaper, August 25th 1894

[66] Sir. J. Ramsay, *Lancaster and York,* Vol II, (Oxford, 1892), pp. 227-230

[67] Eng Chron, p96

[68] Stone, p. 80

[69] Short, p. 74

[70] Benet, p. 226

[71] Hall, p 244

[72] Wavrin, p. 323

[73] D N Hall, *Hardingstone Parish Survey*, Northamptonshire Archaeology, Vol 15, (NAS, 1980) p. 126

[74] Stone, p. 80

[75] Wavrin, BnF fr. 52308, f. 198

[76] Eng Chron, p96. It is this single comment that Ramsay writing in the late 1800's took to mean that the battle was fought actually on the banks of the River Nene. It is a theory that has been followed for many years and it has only been in recent years that it has proved to be most unlikely. Looking across the battlefield from Queen Eleanor's Cross today, it is easy to see that the river could be seen behind the camp.

[77] *Calendar of Close Rolls, Henry VI*: Volume 6, 1454-1461, C. T. Flower (ed.) (HMSO, 1947) p. 450

[78] CSP, p. 27

[79] Six, pp. 150-1

[80] Wavrin pp 295-96. The name that Wavrin gives is *Devistalle, deinstalle* or *demstalle*. fr 20358, f. 197v, has *doustable*. However Wavrin also says they were six miles from Northampton at the time, so may have been closer.

[81] Ibid

[82] *Eng Chron* pp96-7. Whethamstede on the other hand only talks of one rebuff, Whet, pp. 372-4.

[83] Hall, p. 244

[84] *Wavrin* op. cit. pp. 299-300

[85] Ibid

[86] Ibid

[87] Walter C Metcalfe, *Book of Knights Banneret, Knights of the Bath and Knight Batchelor*, (London, 1885) p. 2

[88] Hall, p. 244

[89] *Newsletter from Bruges, 7/15 July 1460, and London, 7/10 July 1460: A Digest*, Quoted in K. Dockray, *Henry VI, Margaret of Anjou and the Wars of the Roses: A Source Book*, (Stroud, 2000) p. 98

[90] Wavrin, pp. 322-24. This account seems to be a report added to the book from another source. It is not in all the early versions.

[91] E.T. Jones, J. Laughton and P. Clark, *Northampton in the Late Middle Ages: Working Paper No. 10*, University of Leicester 2000, pp. 20-23, 37-38

[92] Wavrin, pp. 299-300.

[93] *Eng Chron,* pp. 96-7.

[94] Pius II, *Commentaries* Op. Cit, p.270

[95]
http://www.bandaarcgeophysics.co.uk/arch/roman_marching_camps_uk.html #march_units accessed 20 Sept 2015.

[96] Hall p. 244

[97] Whet, p. 372

[98] Wavrin, pp. 299-300

[99] Unpublished report Glenn Foard, 2015

[100] Whet, pp. 372-4.

[101] Of all the chroniclers mentioned in this chapter, only Gregory's, Gairdner's and Bale's fail to mention Grey.

[102] Beverlac p. 228

[103] Sir H. Ellis (ed), *Three books of Polydore Virgil*, Camden Soc London 1844 p. 107

[104] M. Mercer, *The Medieval Gentry: Power, Leadership and Choice during the Wars of the Roses*, London 2011 P.58

[105] Wavrin, pp 299-300

[106] Eng Chron, pp. 97-8

[107] The 18th century antiquarian John Anstis also named her as "Elizabeth Wayte" (Wake, her later married name?). Michael Hicks in *English Political Culture in the Fifteenth Century*, suggests she was a "young widow" when she met Edward. While it remains unclear whether or not Wayte and Lucy are the same, it is widely believed Lucy was also the mother of Elizabeth Plantagenet (born circa 1464), who married Sir Thomas Lumley in 1477.

[108] *The Itinerary of John Leyland*, Vol 1, (Oxford, 1768) p. 10

[109] Annales, p. 481; Eng Chron pp. 98-99; Gregory, pp. 208-209; Stowe pp. 409

[110] *Report of the Deputy Keeper of Public Records* Vol 37, Part II, (London, 1876) p. 677

[111] P. Sulley, *The Hundred of Wirral* , (Birkenhead, 1889) p.76. The similarity between Clegger and Glegg is too close, and probably explains what really happened.

[112] C. Head, *Pius II and the Wars of the Roses*, Archivium Historiae Pontificae, 8, 1970.

[113] Hall p. 245; Stowe p. 414. The later says he was executed by the commons of Kent in Highgate.

[114] *Archaeologia: or miscellaneous tracts relating to antiquity, Vol XXIX* Society of Antiquaries (London, 1842) pp.334-340

[115] CSP, I 27

[116] C. L. Kingsford, *Prejudice and Promise in Fifteenth Century England* (London, 1962), pp. 54-55

[117] London Chronicle p. 172, Eng Chron, p. 99

[118] Whet, p. 376

[119] *Calendar of Patent Rolls, 1461-1468*, (HMSO, 1897) p. 28

[120] Markham, Op. Cit, pp. 89-90

[121] Hall, p. 274

[122] This includes the contemporary chronicles listed above and http://www.towton.org.uk/wp-content/uploads/database_war_roses_combatants.pdf

Made in the USA
Charleston, SC
17 May 2016